Praise for *Future*

"From P. J. O'Rourke to Deirdre McCloskey, lemonade stands to bitcoin blockchains, uber economics to omniphagic software, the power grid to the connected home, *Future* is a diverse and dynamic cornucopia of historians, futurists, humorists, prophets, and economists discoursing disruptively on the prospects for our 21st Century economy."

> —**George Gilder**, author of *The Scandal of Money* and *Wealth and Poverty*; Founding Fellow, Discovery Institute

"*Future* is exactly what I would expect from the Independent Institute. You will not likely have any sure answers when you finish reading this marvelous book, but I all but guarantee you that you will be asking far better informed questions than at the start. And given the confusing landscape called the future, that's the whole point, isn't it?"

> —**Tom Peters**, Founder and Chairman, Tom Peters Company; author of *In Search of Excellence: Lessons from America's Best Run Companies* (with Robert Waterman, Jr.) and other books

"No one knows what the future will bring, but we do know what policies avert economic calamity and foster widespread prosperity. *Future* provides a roadmap for adopting the essential measures of liberty, entrepreneurship, and innovation. I highly recommend everyone read this pioneering book."

> —**Rand Paul, M.D.**, U.S. Senator

"I predict that the hints of pessimism and caution expressed by the generally optimistic contributors to the book *Future*'s probing examination will all pale in importance relative to the achievements of the ultimate resource: The human mind."

> —**Vernon L. Smith**, Nobel Laureate in Economic Sciences, Chapman University

"Strategic thinking requires understanding of the impact and implications of our present decisions, and predictions for the next fifty years can be a valuable way to critique the state of our world today. The fascinating book *Future* succeeds admirably in provoking and informing about the directions our choices may take us. Those who fail to think about the future are destined to repeat the mistakes of the past!"

> —**Garry K. Kasparov**, Chairman, Human Rights Foundation; 13th World Chess Champion; and author, *Winter Is Coming*

"*Future* is a treasure trove. It demonstrates that sound economic thinking is still alive and teeming with insight, and reminds us that whatever the future brings, it is markets, not state policy, which will best get us there."

    —**David A. Stockman**, former Director, U.S. Office of Management and Budget; former U.S. Congressman

"*Future* is an immensely readable and important book by an All-Star cast of thinkers about what the future may hold for all of us and what we should do now to avert calamity. Agree or disagree with their conclusions, they will make you think deeply about the important topics of freedom, prosperity, and economics."

    —**Peter F. Schweizer**, President, Government Accountability Institute; best-selling author, *Clinton Cash*, *Extortion*, *Throw Them All Out*, and other books

"How can policymakers help the most people build the best lives? Thanks to rapid changes in the structure of our economy and the social fabric that underlies it, that question demands innovative thinking. But too many in the policy community seem content to rely on old arguments and shoehorn new challenges into outmoded paradigms. *Future* is an impressive book from challenging thinkers who invite readers to question their assumptions and look afresh at how markets, technology, and government interact."

    —**Arthur C. Brooks**, President, American Enterprise Institute

"The world around us used to move slowly, hobbled by tradition, guilds and government. Capitalism and more limited government brought faster change, but was still slowed by the State's taxation and controls. Now Technology is allowing consumers and producers to bypass the dead hand of inertia, barriers to entry, and government's efforts to tax and control. *Future* shows how we will be living, learning and earning in the future—a future that has already begun to arrive. Want to know how you will learn, earn and live in the coming decades? This foresightful book outlines the transformation brought by the digital revolution and the coming future that has, in part, already arrived."

    —**Grover G. Norquist**, President, Americans for Tax Reform

FUTURE

INDEPENDENT
I N S T I T U T E

INDEPENDENT INSTITUTE is a non-profit, non-partisan, public-policy research and educational organization that shapes ideas into profound and lasting impact. The mission of Independent is to boldly advance peaceful, prosperous, and free societies grounded in a commitment to human worth and dignity. Applying independent thinking to issues that matter, we create transformational ideas for today's most pressing social and economic challenges. The results of this work are published as books, our quarterly journal, *The Independent Review*, and other publications and form the basis for numerous conference and media programs. By connecting these ideas with organizations and networks, we seek to inspire action that can unleash an era of unparalleled human flourishing at home and around the globe.

100 Swan Way, Oakland, California 94621-1428, U.S.A.
Telephone: 510-632-1366 • Facsimile: 510-568-6040 • Email: info@independent.org • www.independent.org

FUTURE
ECONOMIC PERIL
OR PROSPERITY?

Edited by Robert M. Whaples,
Christopher J. Coyne, and Michael C. Munger

INDEPENDENT
INSTITUTE

OAKLAND, CALIFORNIA

Independent Institute
100 Swan Way, Oakland, CA 94621-1428
Telephone: 510-632-1366
Fax: 510-568-6040
Email: info@independent.org
Website: www.independent.org

Cover Design: Denise Tsui
Cover Image: © 123RF / Iakov Kalinin

Library of Congress Cataloging-in-Publication Data

Names: Coyne, Christopher J., editor. | Munger, Michael C., editor. | Whaples, Robert, editor.
Title: Future : economic peril or prosperity? / edited by Christopher J. Coyne, Michael C Munger, Robert M. Whaples.
Description: Oakland, CA : Independent Institute, 2016. | Includes bibliographical references and index.
Identifiers: LCCN 2015046897 (print) | LCCN 2016005020 (ebook) | ISBN 9781598132748 (hardback) | ISBN 9781598132755 (paperback) | ISBN 9781598132762 (ePub) | ISBN 9781598132786 (Mobi) | ISBN 9781598132779 (Pdf)
Subjects: LCSH: Economic forecasting. | Economic history. | BISAC: BUSINESS & ECONOMICS / Forecasting. | BUSINESS & ECONOMICS / Economic Conditions.
Classification: LCC HB3730 .F88 2016 (print) | LCC HB3730 (ebook) | DDC 330.9001/12--dc23
LC record available at https://lccn.loc.gov/2015046897

Contents

1

The Economic Future

An Introduction

Robert M. Whaples

PREDICTION HAS A venerable tradition among economists. In "Economic Possibilities for Our Grandchildren," John Maynard Keynes—even as the Great Depression was unfolding—famously threw aside the contemporary "attack of economic pessimism" and predicted that a century later the "standard of life" in economically progressive countries would be "between four and eight times as high as it is to-day."[1] History has generally vindicated this optimism. Not that real gross domestic product (GDP) per capita is the only or the best measure of the standard of life, but by this useful metric income per person in the United Kingdom is now more than five times higher than when Keynes wrote his essay,[2] and in the United States it is more than six times higher.[3] These gains look modest in comparison to trends in many developing countries.[4]

Keynes's task was especially challenging. A century is a very long time. Prompted by the birth of my first grandchild last year, I have begun to wonder what life might be like when she reaches my age—roughly fifty years from now. Accordingly, my coeditors, Michael Munger and Christopher Coyne, and I have recruited an intriguing panel of economists (not all with degrees in economics) to help clarify the picture. They all admit that this task is daunting, but they are too modest. Even the skeptical reader will find a profusion of insights in the articles that follow.

As a whole—like Keynes and other economists who have answered this question—our panelists are generally optimistic, although the optimism is carefully guarded in some cases. This optimism accords with the broader opinion held by economists surveyed about a decade ago,[5] although the intervening ten years of disappointing economic performance appears to have tempered it a bit. That survey asked randomly selected members of the American Economic Association (AEA) to predict the growth in per capita income in the United States over the next sixty years; the median response was that growth would be "positive but slightly less than the rate over the past sixty years," which was fairly robust.[6] Such a growth rate would imply an increase in average incomes of about 150 percent in the next fifty years. There is similar optimism among most of the authors in the collected volume *In 100 Years: Leading Economists Predict the Future*,[7] whose first chapter identifies one obvious historical trend as "unrelenting growth" and concludes that, "absent a major move away from inclusive institutions at the world level, our grandchildren should also be writing about how unrelenting growth has been in their past century."[8] Another of these leading economists predicts that by 2113 "we will have managed . . . to completely eliminate [absolute] poverty in the world."[9]

The reasons for economic optimism are abundant but can be boiled down to the fact that economists expect technology will continue to improve provided that reasonable economic incentives to encourage this discovery and to implement its fruits persist. The predicted changes range from innocent innovations that will make life a bit more comfortable (such as the pillow that learns your sleep rhythms partnered with the coffee maker that knows when you have awakened—see Lynne Kiesling's essay) to potentially chilling technologies that might strip our human dignity (including the almost complete elimination of privacy and electronic supplementation of the brain embedded in a government controlled educational system—see Charlotte Twight's essay).

I won't spoil the surprises you'll find in these thoughtful and immensely readable essays, but because none of our authors has room to explore the broad technological horizon in much detail, I consider here the historical trends in total factor productivity, and then survey some of the technologies that might revolutionize the economy in the coming half-century. Economic historian Alexander Field[10] estimates that the growth of total factor productivity—the ability to turn inputs into output—for the private domestic economy was fairly rapid in the late 1800s, declined somewhat in the years before and during World War I, reached its peak in the period from 1919 to 1973 (with a noticeable hiatus during World War II), and slowed dramatically in the final decades of the twentieth century, before picking up again after that.[11] He argues that the first surge of productivity growth was tied to the implementation of steam-engine technology in factories and transportation; the second wave was driven by electrification and the internal combustion engine; and—after a pause—the third wave has been due to computers and related technologies.

Unfortunately, the most recent total factor productivity growth rate pales in comparison to that of the earlier golden age. This discrepancy has led economists such as Tyler Cowen[12] to argue that we have already picked the "low-hanging fruit"—we have made the easy discoveries—making future discoveries much harder to obtain, so "average is over." Sharing this "pessimism"—although this is not quite the right word because the argument is that growth will slow but not completely stop or reverse any time soon—is Robert Gordon, who attacks "the assumption, nearly universal since [Robert] Solow's seminal contributions of the 1950s, that economic growth is a continuous process that will persist forever. . . . Rather, the rapid progress made over the past 250 years could well turn out to be a unique episode in human history."[13] "After a century of life-changing innovations that spurred growth," predicts Gordon, "human progress is slowing to a crawl."[14]

In contrast, the majority view among economists sees far more potential in the next wave (or waves) of technology. One source of this optimism is that rising population will boost the number of scientists, engineers, and entrepreneurs around the world who work to push out the technological frontier. More people equals more brains, and those brains will continue to become better educated in science and technology, especially with the economic rise of Asia. The number of master's degrees in engineering and technology awarded in China has soared in the past two decades, surpassing the U.S. total in 2004, and—if trends continue—the figures for India will soon move it ahead of the U.S. total, too.[15] Likewise, research and development spending in East Asia pulled even with levels in North America in 2011[16] and will inevitably dwarf the amount spent in North America, swelling the global total. Spurring this process, the payoff from innovation will undoubtedly grow as markets continue to globalize. History suggests that almost all the gains from technological progress ultimately go to consumers all around the world, not to producers.

Technological possibilities (probabilities?) are rife throughout the entire economy. Healthcare is the largest sector in the United States. Within the next half-century, breakthroughs in the understanding of biology and the application of computers promise to continue the extension of life, wipe out old diseases (including malaria, tuberculosis, AIDS, and perhaps even obesity), fight disease in new ways (such as computers in the blood stream), and build personalized replacement body tissues and organs. They may even begin the merger of human and machine and widespread usage of drugs and genetic engineering to enhance memory, intelligence, and physical abilities—not just for those who are disabled and sick but for everyone. (These ideas are potentially scary.) Breakthroughs in energy hold the promise of making fossil fuels obsolete. The inflation-adjusted cost of solar power has plunged, as has the cost of battery storage (which is vital for making solar energy competitive with natural gas), bringing down the overall cost of solar power about 75 percent since 2000. If current trends continue, optimists predict that by 2030 solar power will be cheaper than fossil fuel power from the grid even in not-so-sunny places.[17] By 2065, a massive transition seems inevitable—unless, of course, breakthroughs in fossil fuels come even faster than in alternative fuels. Consider other natural resources. The mining of asteroids is on the near-term horizon.[18] Rapid improvements in desalination technology could make freshwater scarcity a problem of the past. Even if agriculture merely continues to use current technologies to modify crops, their yields will continue to rise, and breakthroughs could make food even more plentiful. Manufacturing is ripe for major changes based on three-dimensional printers. And robotization will diffuse throughout manufacturing and into the rest of the economy.[19]

Some of the most important new technologies will probably happen in transportation. In *Back to the Future Part II*,[20] Marty McFly travels to 2015 and shows a couple of kids how to play a video game from the 1980s. Their dismissive reply is, "You mean you have to use your hands? That's like a baby's toy." In 2065, will anyone still use their hands to drive an automobile? Driverless cars are already on our roads, and their advent will likely lead to a huge economic reconfiguration. Because autonomous vehicles will be able to move safely at much higher speeds, cities will be redesigned. You won't need an Uber driver to shuttle you. A driverless car—which you may or may not own—will pick you up and drop you off, allowing you to travel while you're busy doing something else (e.g., working, playing, socializing, nursing a hangover, star gazing), tired, or even asleep. (Cars might become mobile hotel rooms.) This could mean suburban "sprawl"—an ugly name for a benign process—on steroids. The car could take the kids to Grandma's house and bring them back home again. Whatever goes for cars, goes for trucks, too. Similarly, drones might be everywhere (if we want them to be), changing delivery patterns.

The list goes on and on.

Will the rate of technological progress slow down? When I suggest this to college students, they tend to let out an audible snort or roll their eyes and emphatically dismiss the very idea—especially those who study science and technology.

Yet the authors in our symposium raise a number of important cautions concerning forces that might derail or at least decelerate technologically driven economic growth. At the top of the list is rising government debt due to spiraling entitlement spending. The issues they raise mirror the major concerns expressed by members of the AEA a decade ago. In that survey, I asked respondents to list the "three most important economic challenges facing the United States over the next sixty years." Their most important worries included problems caused by aging, Social Security, and pensions (listed by 50 percent of respondents); healthcare and insurance (34.3 percent); and education (24.3 percent).[21] Another persistent concern among the authors who have contributed to our symposium is creeping government power and regulations that stifle economic initiative. Bruce Yandle[22] warns of the choking stranglehold of this kudzulike growth of government regulation. Why so many laws and regulations? Perhaps Tacitus had it right in warning that "[c]orruptissima re publica plurimae leges"[23]—the more numerous the laws, the more corrupt the government. The causation seems to run both ways.

It may strike some as odd that *none* of our authors raises the issue of global climate change. However, this result matches well with the earlier survey of general economists, in which only 17.1 percent listed environmental problems as a top worry, and only 4.2 percent explicitly mentioned climate change. In another survey, I asked economists, "In comparison to a world in which greenhouse gas levels were stable, rising levels of greenhouse gases by the end of the twenty-first century will cause GDP per capita in the U.S. to be [how much lower or higher]?" The most popular response was "less than 1 percent lower or higher."[24] My sense is that most economists don't see global climate change as a looming problem mainly because they believe that the economy is fairly flexible and that the "ultimate resource," human ingenuity, will mitigate problems (if they ever arrive) with fairly inexpensive fixes, which may include geoengineering. There may also be skepticism that temperatures will rise as much as the Intergovernmental Panel on Climate Change predicts.

But there are some kinds of problems that science and technology cannot solve—and some they can make worse. Relentless economic growth may mean that the problems faced by most people around the world will increasingly be "First World problems." Among the complaints "Weird Al" Yankovic[25] makes in his parody song "First World Problems" are that he has too many groceries for his gigantic refrigerator; he can't remember which car he has driven to the mall; his electric toothbrush won't recharge, so he has to brush his teeth "like a Neanderthal"; and his house is so big he can't get a WiFi connection in the kitchen. These are problems of excess—gluttony and selfishness—that technology can't fix.

Will our almost inevitable economic progress make most people truly better off? I have considerable doubts, which partially hinge on the fact that more isn't always better—especially when you already have enough. For example, despite considerable economic growth, subjective well-being among Americans has not risen during the past four decades[26] and has apparently declined somewhat for women. The argument can be made that this plateauing has been caused by worsening noneconomic factors (such as the impact of divorce)[27] that have cancelled out the potentially benign impact of rising levels of real income. However, it may be that income above a certain level has no power to increase genuine well-being (for example, Arthur Brooks[28] sees no real gains past an income of $75,000 per year).[29]

With this in mind, let me add two deep concerns I have about our economic future. The first problem is that the erosion of marriage and the family may increasingly harm us. Shelly Lundberg and Robert A. Pollak[30] document this trend, showing the share of thirty- to forty-four-year-old men currently married dropping from 85 percent in 1950 to 60 percent in 2010 and the drop for was women nearly as large. The decline in the proportion of the population that is married has been especially strong for those with less education. Simultaneously, births to nonmarried couples as a proportion of all births rose from 5 percent in 1959 to 53 percent in 2011. Lundberg and Pollak argue that broad economic changes—especially increased employment opportunities for women—are largely responsible for this pattern as the gains from specialization by couples have disappeared. They argue that marriage has declined less among well-educated couples because it serves as a commitment mechanism that supports high levels of investment in children and is hence more valuable for couples adopting a high-investment strategy for their children. Unless the goal is to raise high-achieving children, then, more and more women feel that they don't need a husband, and more and more men feel that they don't need a wife. In 2014, the U.S. census estimated that 27 percent of all children lived in a fatherless home, and another census study estimates that in 2009 just 59 percent of all American children lived with their married and biological parents.[31]

Although women might not need husbands as much, their children—especially their male children—do seem to benefit greatly from having their fathers around.[32] Joel Schwartz[33] documents that marriage substantially reduces childhood poverty rates and infant mortality rates and that, holding other factors constant, boys raised in single-parent homes are about twice as likely to have committed a crime that leads to incarceration by the time they reach their early thirties. The impact appears to carry over to the labor market. W. Bradford Wilcox and Robert I. Lerman estimate that almost 40 percent of the decline in male employment since 1979 arose because of the drop in the number of intact families.[34]

Even if the economic forces driving the disintegration of families were to disappear, the decline of parenting may get much worse in the future as women follow men in losing their taste for parenthood. The total fertility rate in the United States has fallen below the replacement level, reaching 1.88 children born per woman in 2012.[35] This trend is part of what Nicholas Eberstadt calls "the global flight from the family," which he attributes to "the seemingly unstoppable quest for convenience by adults demanding ever-greater autonomy."[36] This "flight from the family" is seen not merely in Europe but also in Asia (e.g., 30 percent of Hong Kong's women in their early forties are childless) and even in the Middle East (e.g., nearly 32 percent of Libyan women in their late thirties are unmarried). This "triumph" of consumer sovereignty makes it "easier than ever before to free oneself from the burdens that would otherwise be imposed by spouses, children, relatives, or significant others"[37] and is likely to increase in the future due to new technologies, distractions, and attitudes.[38]

A declining fertility level (which has fallen all the way to 0.8 children born per woman in Hong Kong) and the consequent aging of society could be a huge drag on the economy all by themselves. But the impact of children being raised without two parents might be even worse. Will the values inculcated in well-functioning families, the values that make economies and societies flourish—such as how to support dependents and not remain one into adulthood—wither away? Jonathan Sacks predicts that the "Western abandonment of marriage will go down in history as one of the tragic instances of what Friedrich Hayek called 'the fatal conceit' that somehow we know better than the wisdom of the ages" and observes that "[marriage] is where one generation passes on its values to the next, ensuring the continuity of a civilization."[39]

My second big worry about the future is that complacency will become a normal good. As we get richer, we can afford to ignore problems around us, including the degeneration of the very idea of freedom. J. Budziszewski puts it this way: "First[,] freedom meant our noble power of rational and moral self-direction. Then it meant the mere absence of restraints on our will, so long as we were not violating moral law. Then it meant the absence of any restraints whatsoever. Finally it meant the sheer power to act immorally and irrationally, even if the power of rational and moral self-direction were taken from us."[40] Americans seem to have lost most of the earlier, true definition of freedom, and the trend seems likely to continue. This trend may or may not affect our rate of economic growth, but it certainly will affect the ends to which we put our burgeoning economic powers and may reshape the economy in hideous ways. One significant effect might be a ratcheting up of governmental power as we continue to unlearn how free men and women act.[41]

I suspect that if asked fifty years ago about the future of the economy, most economists would have given answers similar to those provided by the economists in this symposium. They would have been broadly optimistic but would have pointed out problems that might arise to stall the engine. They may have mentioned problems such as nuclear war, the depletion of natural resources, and overpopulation and starvation in developing countries, without foreseeing some major changes in the world, including the end of the Cold War, the economic rise of China, and the Internet. Their nightmare scenarios didn't unfold; instead, things turned out mostly better than these economists probably would have expected. May we be so blessed.

2

From Lemonade Stands to 2065

Pierre Lemieux

ONE PROBLEM WITH predicting the future is that it is full of surprises, which by definition are impossible to predict. Another problem is that the forecaster, to the extent that he feels capable of influencing events, is tempted by wishful thinking: to predict what he wishes to happen. Ecologists of the 1960s and 1970s were especially adept at that, predicting mass starvation within a few decades.[1] In this short essay, I focus mainly on the United States, although my tea leaves also reveal something about the rest of the world. I try in turn (1) to build a simple forecast of the standard of living, (2) to explore a neglected megatrend, (3) to look at surprises that might further affect the world before 2065, and (4) to reorganize all these factors around two possible polar worlds. In the process, to separate the normative from the positive, I propose a criterion for distinguishing between good (or better) and bad (or worse) scenarios.

Simple Predictions about Gross Domestic Product

Surprisingly, simple predictions of the standard of living often seem to get it right. In 1930, John Maynard Keynes predicted that the standard of living would multiply by between four and eight times over the following one hundred years.[2] If we measure the standard of living with real gross domestic product (GDP) per capita (which is the most general measure of average income), Keynes was quite on the mark: from 1930 to 2014, the actual increase of real GDP per capita was more than sixfold, and there are still sixteen of his one hundred years to go. This growth occurred despite a world war and the recent Great Recession—showing how resilient a more or less free economy

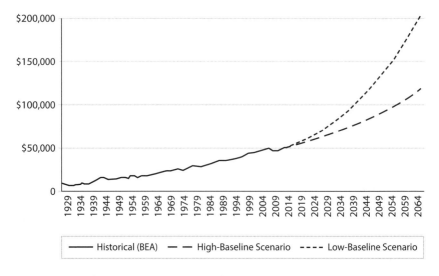

Figure 2.1. Real GDP per Capita, United States, 1929–2065

is. Similarly, the predictions of the late futurists Herman Kahn and Anthony Wiener were pretty close to the mark. In 1967, they provided forecasts for real GDP per capita in the year 2000. The actual figure turned out to be close to the midpoint between their most optimistic and most pessimistic predictions, which ranged between a twofold and a fourfold increase.

Figure 1 attempts a similar simple forecasting exercise for the U.S. economy fifty years from now. My high-baseline scenario would have real GDP per capita grow at 2.8 percent per year, which corresponds to the growth rate between 1930 and 1973. My low-baseline scenario would see an annual growth of 1.7 percent, the growth rate experienced since 1973. The lower growth can be thought of as representing what some analysts describe as the new "Great Stagnation." My low-baseline scenario is close to the forecast made by the U.S. Congressional Budget Office (CBO), which envisions a growth rate of 1.6 percent over the next seventy-five years.[3] This suggests that my low-baseline scenario may be a bit optimistic.

Because of compounding, the end result of either of my two scenarios translates into significant increases in the standard of living: by 2065, real GDP per capita would have been multiplied by a factor between 2.3 and 4.1, depending on which scenario obtains. To grasp what this means, imagine your real income either doubling or quadrupling.

My two baseline scenarios can be interpreted as reflecting two different paths of regulation. A good argument can be made that economic growth is positively affected by economic freedom (and attendant institutions) and negatively impacted by the opposite of economic freedom, regulation.[4] Between 1949 and 2005, the Code of Federal Regulations was multiplied sixfold to more than 134,000 pages.[5] Charles Murray counted 175,000 pages for 2012.[6] These pages do not include state and local regulations. One can argue that the rapid growth of regulation after World War II has played a major role in the slowdown of economic growth.[7] My low-baseline scenario can be thought of as incorporating the impact of the regulation explosion, my high-baseline scenario as the growth potential if the postwar regulatory explosion were dowsed. In other words, my high-growth scenario assumes a decrease of regulation, whereas my low-growth scenario assumes some leveling off in the regulatory trend.

Although comparable data are missing, it is certainly true that the regulation explosion started not with the end of World War II but with the New Deal and that it was smoldering for a few decades before that. Only the resilience of markets in an entrepreneurial economy can probably explain the relatively high growth rates that persisted until a few decades ago. Moreover, the damage caused by regulation—its marginal cost—certainly increases with its volume, which would explain why the Great Stagnation did not become visible earlier.[8] The Great Stagnation is probably the result of this whole regulatory megatrend.

The Regulatory Megatrend

The impact of the regulatory megatrend is the most important and the most neglected factor in understanding the world we live in. How regulation evolves will play a major role in what the economy and society will look like in fifty years' time.

Nearly two centuries ago, Alexis de Tocqueville forecasted this regulatory megatrend and imagined the democratic dystopia of the future. The sovereign power, he thought, would extend its reach "over the whole community" and seek "to fix [men] in perpetual childhood." "It attends to their security, provides for their needs, facilitates their pleasures, conducts their principal affairs, directs their industry." It "covers the surface of society with a network of small, complicated, minute, and uniform rules. . . . [I]t does not break wills, but it softens them, bends them. . . . [I]t does not tyrannize, it hinders, it represses, it enervates, it extinguishes, it stupefies, and finally it reduces each nation to being nothing more than a flock of timid and industrious animals, of which the government is the shepherd."[9]

Without claiming to be exhaustive, I suggest that if the regulatory megatrend continues unabated, its results in half a century may be summarized by three metaphors.

The Central-Bank Metaphor. The "small, complicated, minute" regulations forecasted by Tocqueville cannot suffer the straightjacket of uniform rules. They have to escape the rule of law as the concept used to be known. To regulate or even to monitor everything, discretion and arbitrariness become necessary. Powerful central agencies with wide power and discretion are required. We can call this process the "central-bank model,"[10] although several other federal agencies fit the model well. According to this perspective, the politicians of the future will be content to establish and occasionally tweak powerful independent agencies. In practice, the latter will be the real legislator. Continuous electronic democracy, if it were implemented, might interfere with this setup, but it would mainly add more whim and inconsistency.

The Parenting-License Metaphor. Not only narrowly defined economic activities will be hit. In today's world, permits and licenses are already needed to do many things, including to operate children's lemonade stands.[11] Strangely, however, no permit is needed for conceiving and raising children, activities that produce more consequential externalities than selling lemonade, driving a clunker, or operating a massage clinic. If the regulatory megatrend continues, this incongruity will be corrected with the establishment of a parenting license.[12]

The Travel Metaphor. Continuous surveillance is indispensable to minute regulation. By 2065, all conversations, emails, and physical letters will be scanned and kept in databases, where the authorities can retrieve them, perhaps with special warrants issued by special courts. All encryption software will automatically provide some government agency with a private key (or another sort of "backdoor"). Any nonlocal trip (longer than, say, one hundred miles) will need to be logged on a government website. Of course, drivers' licenses will have completed their transformation into a national ID card long before 2065; it has already happened for all practical purposes, with only a central database missing.

That the continuation of the regulatory megatrend will still produce a 1.7 percent annual real growth (as in my low-baseline scenario) may again seem overly optimistic, but one must not forget how resilient markets are, even when constrained. Asia provides some examples, although sustaining high-growth rates is easier at lower stages of development. We can expect technological progress to exert an upward pressure on GDP, canceling part of the negative impact of regulation.

GDP tells only part of the story. Although there exists a close correlation between income and welfare,[13] individuals' goal is the latter, not the former, and the two variables can sometimes move in different directions. For example, the fast growth of GDP during World War II did not equate with an increase in welfare (at least in the short run or for the dead coerced conscripts). If we want to evaluate our economic future and not "simply" forecast it, we should ultimately be interested in individual welfare.

Measuring welfare, even only conceptually, opens a huge Pandora's box. I propose to sidestep the problem by assuming that individual liberty, properly defined, is an important part of any individual's welfare not only because it exerts a direct influence on GDP but also because it is by itself an argument in most if not all individuals' utility functions—an idea that the Western political tradition owes to the eighteenth century. So we should also be interested in the state of individual liberty fifty years from now. I will thus use liberty as my main normative criterion.

Regulation generally constrains liberty. The only exception would be when it is required to produce public goods and protect liberty itself. The Tocquevillian regulation that has developed in the past several decades is quite certainly not of that sort, and only a small number of the 4,500 federal statutes on the books in 2007[14] protect everybody's liberty. It follows that my high-baseline scenario, which implies some (and probably much) deregulation, means a higher level of individual liberty than today and that my low-baseline scenario, which incorporates a great deal of regulation, must result in a lower level of individual liberty. Anybody who agrees that liberty is a normative criterion thus has another reason to prefer the high-baseline scenario to the low-baseline scenario.

Global Surprises

Surprises—that is, significant unexpected events—will also influence the state of America and the world in fifty years' time. What these surprises will be, nobody knows, but we can try to peek under the hood of the future. On the basis of the evaluation criteria suggested earlier, these surprises will be either good or bad depending primarily on their effect on individual liberty (and secondarily on incomes).

Surprises can be either physical/biological or social/economic/political. The former include severe pandemics, perhaps with antibiotic resistance, massive volcanic eruptions, collisions with large asteroids, crippling solar geomagnetic storms, and so on.[15] The disruptive potential of such events is large: they could push America below my low-baseline scenario and lead governments in all countries to dramatically restrict liberties. However, the probability of these catastrophes is low.

Man-made surprises can be good or bad. It may be inspiring to look at half a dozen such surprises that over the past fifty years have had global significance. Which surprises would an observer in the mid-1960s have been less likely to forecast? Six candidates (in no particular order) are (1) China's economic take-off and rapid growth, at least under the form it has taken; (2) the Internet; (3) the terrorist attacks of September 11, 2001, and the return of religious wars (brought about by Islam); (4) widespread government surveillance in the United States; (5) the disintegration of the Soviet Union; and (6) the questioning of free speech in the West (including free-speech codes and "triggerism" in American universities as well as hate-speech laws in other countries).

These events were difficult to forecast either because they clashed head on with what appeared to be major trends or generalized beliefs at the time (numbers 3 to 6) or because they pushed existing trends far beyond their imagined paths (numbers 1 and 2). Kahn and Wiener[16] gave a glimpse at the possibility of numbers 1, 2, and 4, but even in these cases the future developed in its own sneaky way.

Similar black swans for the next fifty years, on both the good and the bad sides, might figure in the following list:

Free trade or autarky. Good surprise: One major country declares unilateral free trade, leading to a general drop in protectionism. **Bad surprise**: Protectionism and autarky spread worldwide, perhaps as a response to some other catastrophe.

Leisure society or new Luddism. Good surprise: Something close to machine intelligence is achieved, leading to the leisure society that theorists have been predicting for decades.[17] Or there might be another, more realistic sort of major technological advance. **Bad surprise**: Luddite revolts spread, perhaps after a technological accident.

Resistance or nuclear war. Good surprise: Some new technology dramatically increases individuals' capacity to resist tyranny. **Bad surprise**: A nuclear war causes devastating damage and deaths.

Liberty restored in the United States or tyranny established. Good surprise: A vast movement rebuilds American liberty, perhaps as Charles Murray[18] advocates. **Bad surprise**: A world government is instituted, possibly in the aftermath of nuclear war. Alternatively, a dictatorship is established in the United States or in other major countries of the West.

Some states (nearly) wither away, or the United States crashes. Good surprise: Nonstate organizations develop to the point where the usefulness of the state is questioned in the United States and elsewhere in the world. Perhaps some states are replaced by minimum states. **Bad surprise**: A severe economic crash occurs in the United States, perhaps following defaults on public debt and hyperinflation.[19] Or political polarization leads to a new civil war and the dissolution of the union. (In case of disintegration, some parts of the former country may reestablish liberty and thrive, which would be a good surprise from the point of view of most individuals living there.)

Two Alternative Polar Worlds

By construction, good surprises will increase individual liberty; bad ones will decrease it. The impact on GDP should be in the same direction. My high-baseline and low-baseline scenarios would be amplified. Nobody knows if we can expect more good or bad surprises. But we may be in a position to reformulate our two simple scenarios into something more complete. In this section, I try to combine in two polar worlds the different strands of thought I have pursued: the two simple GDP scenarios, the regulatory megatrend, and the possible surprises that can mitigate or exaggerate these developments. The two polar worlds that might exist in year 2065 are very different.

If we assume the continuation of the regulatory megatrend and a larger probability of bad surprises, the prognosis is not good. Our grandchildren will be lucky to get the low-baseline scenario for economic growth and will live in a much less free world. This bad polar world may look very much like the caring tyranny of Aldous Huxley's novel *Brave New World* (1932) or George Lucas's film *THX-1138* (1971). A more cruel tyranny à la George Orwell's *Nineteen Eighty-Four* (1949) is less probable but might develop after a major catastrophe. The developing police abuse in the United States gives us some insider hints. The only hope in the bad polar world would be that there remain some spaces, physical or virtual, where some individual liberty survives. This hope would be reduced by the creation of a world government.

At this point, the parallelism I proposed between liberty and welfare may completely break down. Most people may well enjoy their golden chains. Except perhaps for the elderly, they will never have experienced anything else. James Buchanan[20] called "parentalism" the desire of people to be taken care of by the state, like children by their parents, and he forecasted that this phenomenon would continue to fuel socialism in the twenty-first century. The parentalist society is very close to the Huxley–Lucas version of my bad polar world.

My crystal ball has a murky area that I have not explored, in part because it does not fit with Tocqueville's egalitarian forecasts. But it ties in well with the class vision of *Brave New World*. In this version of the bad polar world, incomes earned in 2065 will be grossly unequal, extending a phenomenon that seems to be currently emerging. On one side, the lucky, educated, and "law abiding" will be rich and comfortable and obtain permits easily. The earth will belong to them. On the other side, a minority of unlucky, poorly educated, and unpopular individuals will be excluded from many ordinary rights and opportunities. They will be the wretched of the golden earth. Although the state will conspicuously assist these new proletarians, its laws and regulations will be the main cause of their degradation. A prefiguration of this world can be seen in the number of convicted felons (9 percent of American adults, according to estimates by Sarah Shannon and her colleagues),[21] who are often guilty of mere regulatory crimes, can never become "law abiding" again, and find themselves irremediably blocked from many ways to earn a living. We don't know who will be the hated minorities of the future.

The alternative world, the good polar world, assumes that regulation is drastically reduced and that mostly good surprises happen and mankind is spared the most devastating ones. If new technologies can fuel government surveillance and control, they can also undermine regulation (the taxi industry provides a current example). In the good polar world of 2065, we expect a rate of growth at least equal to that of my high-baseline scenario and perhaps much higher. Compounding would again work its magic: for example, if real GDP per capita were to grow at 4 percent per year, it will be multiplied by seven from 2014 to 2065. The average American will then earn an income that makes him rich enough to qualify as a member of today's richest 1 or 2 percent. More important, our grandchildren will be living in a free society.

The future will tell if my good polar world is just wishful thinking.

3

Pessimistically Optimistic about the Future

Peter J. Boettke[*]

AT FIFTY-FIVE YEARS of age and having been a professional economist for thirty years, I am pessimistically optimistic about our economic future. My bottom line is optimistic because, like the great Julian Simon,[1] I believe that the ultimate resource is the human imagination and that the great diversity of human ingenuity and creativity will help us find our way out of the numerous troubles that we have made and may make for ourselves. But I am pessimistically optimistic because the dominant mental models that human beings deploy to make sense of their interaction with each other and with nature are so fundamentally flawed and grounded in zero-sum and negative-sum moral intuitions.

We systematically underestimate the costs of blocking trading opportunities with one another and of curtailing the creative powers of the entrepreneurial spirit, and we systematically overstate the benefits of attempting to curb the excesses of self-interest through collective action by state power. I am an optimist because of the creativity of individuals and the power of the market; I am a pessimist because of the moral intuitions hard-wired into humans through our evolutionary past in small-group settings and the tyranny of government controls in the affairs of men. The logical outcomes of both are fundamentally opposed: complete and unregulated trade with all or isolation and war against all. Human history, I contend, can be seen as the long drama of these two forces battling it out to determine which norms of interaction will be dominant. Put another way, we can follow the Smithian propensity to truck, barter, and exchange, or we can follow the Hobbesian propensity to

*Acknowledgments: I gratefully acknowledge the comments from Christopher Coyne on an earlier draft. The usual caveat applies.

rape, pillage, and plunder. Optimism comes from Smithian propensities winning out over Hobbesian ones, whereas pessimism comes from the Hobbesian propensities sweeping aside the Smithian ones.

Which force will ultimately determine our future path will be a function of ideas. Economic logic and reality are not subject to popular vote any more than the law of gravity or the physical laws governing the flow of water in a river. Reality simply is not optional. But politicians, pundits, and the public often communicate a message as if economic policy is a question of popular will. There is no doubt that populations can vote for this or that economic policy, but whether the policy decided on will have the intended desirable consequences is not a matter of good wishes. Policy effectiveness is a consequence of recognizing the relevant trade-offs that individuals face in their decisions about the utilization of scarce resources and pursuing the opportunities for gains from trade and gains from entrepreneurial innovation.

Certain policies are compatible with realizing productive specialization and peaceful cooperation, and others are not. Bad ideas about humans and nature produce bad public policies about the way humans interact with each other and with nature, which in turn have bad economic results. In contrast, good ideas lead to good policies, which in turn produce good results. The economic miracle of the Western world was a by-product of ideas and institutions that produced high-powered incentives, quality informational signals, and disciplining feedback so that the gains from social cooperation under the division of labor were realized. The lingering poverty in much of the world is a result of ideas and institutions that prevent the realization of gains from social cooperation.

As we contemplate the future of economic policy, the questions we must ask are: Which ideas and institutions will prevail? Are we looking at a future where property, contract, and consent will be foundational to the social order? Or will our future be one where ideas that challenge the very legitimacy of property, deny the freedom of contract, and claim that consent is but an illusion ultimately define the conventional wisdom of the age? Tomorrow will be better than today provided that property, contract, and consent remain pivotal ideas in the social order—that is, the rights of others are respected, promises are kept, and those rights are exchanged or those promises are modified only if both parties agree to the transfer or modification.

We are very imperfect beings who interact with each other in a very imperfect world, but our institutional environments aid us in stumbling our way through to a better world. As Adam Smith remarked in *The Wealth of Nations*, "The natural effort of every individual to better his own condition, when suffered to exert itself with freedom and security, is so powerful a principle, that it is alone, and without any assistance, not only capable of carrying on the society to wealth and prosperity, but of surmounting a hundred impertinent obstructions with which the folly of human laws too often incumbers its operation."[2] For our purposes, at least two aspects of this Smithian claim must be addressed. The first is the business of what it means to exert our individual initiative with freedom and security. The second is the possibility of identifying a tipping point when those impertinent obstructions simply cannot be surmounted.

By stating things in this way, I think, we can begin to identify the probability of whether our future will be bleak because we eliminate the individual's freedom to choose and in so doing adopt not a hundred obstructions to market transactions but hundreds of thousands. What is the probability that the United States will follow a policy path that will kill the proverbial goose that lays the golden egg, as happened in the socialist experiments of the twentieth century in the Soviet Union and China or as experienced in the past decade in Venezuela and Greece? For the democratic West, I say the probability is extremely low, for reasons discussed later, so my pessimism is constrained to the observation that we will continue to muddle through with some form of crony capitalism or mercantilism. Our wealth will not be what it could be. We will continue to suffer from macrovolatility and microdistortions, but the erring entrepreneurs will outpace the bumbling bureaucrats in realizing mutually beneficial exchanges and coming up with creative entrepreneurial innovations in production and distribution of goods and services. We will, as Smith argued, be carried to wealth and prosperity even in the face of the impertinence of human folly motivated by the wrong moral intuitions and the meddlesome preferences of those who hope to lord over others.

To communicate this point to audiences, I have often asked them to envision a horse race between three horses: (1) a Smithian horse representing the gains from exchange, (2) a Schumpeterian horse representing the gains from innovation, and (3) a Stupid horse representing government meddling in the voluntary affairs of humans in the effort to control the economy. As long as the Smith and Schumpeter horses are outrunning the Stupid horse, the economy will continue to progress despite the restrictions under which it must operate. But if we ever allow the Stupid horse not only to gain ground on the Smithian and Schumpeterian horses by shackling them with restrictions on trade and regulations on innovation but also to overcome them, then our economic future will indeed be bleak. The United States isn't at that stage yet, but it might reach that stage if right reason is rejected and emotional appeals substitute for logic and evidence.

Stupidity gains ground if and only if an alliance is forged between wrong ideas and opportunistic political interests. So the economist's task is to debunk popular fallacies and expose the special interests that benefit from the bad policies at the expense of the general populace. Economists must be forever vigilant in their role as public educators—both in and out of the classroom. As I said before, economic reality is not optional—voting for any economic policy by democratic majority does not mean it is a good policy. The worthiness of economic policy measures can be determined on the basis of only one criteria: Do the economic policies proposed result in wealth and prosperity or not? The answer is not arrived at through democratic procedures but through the science of economics and the art of political economy.

In the future, many possible factors will impact the world of affairs—war is perhaps the most obvious, but there are also natural disasters such as earthquakes and hurricanes. But even in the face of these factors, the critical variable under our command is public-policy responses. We should not compound the fury of nature, for example, with the folly of the human being. The policies of economic freedom will dampen the calls for war as trading partners seek to avoid such costly engagements, whereas economic nationalism tends to breed war. In a probabilistic sense, the likelihood of a major war between the Western democratic states is negligible, and thus the biggest threat to our economic future rests with bad ideas and meddlesome preferences. This means we muddle through, confronting not only periodic volatility and distortions wrought by perverse incentives but also episodic technological breakthroughs and innovations in exchange and production as well as the opening up of new markets, both foreign and domestic.

The great political economist James Buchanan often described himself as a pessimist when he looked to the future but an optimist when he looked back because surely the world should be worse off than what it is. My position is slightly different and might be characterized as "pessimistic optimism." As I said, my optimism is grounded in the force of argument from Adam Smith to Julian Simon about the creative forces of the human imagination. My pessimism is equally grounded in the force of argument from Thomas Hobbes to James Buchanan about the war of all against all and the self-serving capacity of political interests. Squeeze these intellectual arguments together—Smith and Hobbes, Simon and Buchanan—and what you get is optimism about productive specialization and peaceful cooperation being realized by diverse populations plus a tempered pessimism due to the desire of many to rule over others and the attempt to control the economy. The upshot is that the economic future of my grandchildren will be bright compared to the world we live in today. But it will not be the post-scarcity world envisioned by Keynes or the apocalyptic future envisioned by many conservatives. Instead, it will be a better world than today, but not as good a world as it could have been had individuals come to understand the tyranny of politics and ineffectiveness of economic policies of control and been more receptive to freedom of choice and the power of the market.

4

The Economy in 2065

Predictions and Cautions

David R. Henderson

There is a great deal of ruin in a nation.
—Adam Smith, qtd. in John Rae, *Life of Adam Smith*[1]

"PREDICTION IS VERY DIFFICULT," said the late Danish physicist Niels Bohr, "especially if it's about the future." He could have added, "And even more so for the distant future." In economic terms, fifty years is the distant future. For that reason, I do not put a large weight on predictions about what the world economy and the U.S. economy will look like in fifty years.

Having said that, I am willing to make some reasonably confident predictions about the future. I follow these predictions with reasons why I have made them.

Predictions

Here are my predictions:

1. World population, currently at about 7.2 billion, will have reached 10 billion before 2065 and will not be higher in 2065. In other words, the world population will have stopped growing.
2. The world economy, measured in real gross domestic product (GDP), will be at least three times as big as it is now owing mainly to productivity growth, not to population growth.
3. The largest economy in the world, measured by real GDP, will be that of China, and its economy will be at least double the size of the U.S. economy.

4. U.S. real GDP will be at least twice what it is now owing mainly to productivity growth, not to population growth.

5. The absolute number of people in the world who are in extreme poverty will be less than half of the number today.

6. In the United States, the average number of hours worked per year for people with jobs will be about 10 percent lower than it is now.

7. A weighted average of a broad range of fuel and mineral prices will not be more than 10 percent higher than it is now.

8. Federal government spending in the United States will be between 20 and 25 percent of GDP.

9. Economic freedom in the United States, as measured by the Economic Freedom Index, currently showing that the United States is number 12 out of 152 countries ranked, will show (if the index is still computed in 2065) that the United States is at or slightly below twentieth place.

Now to my reasons.

Reasons

Population

The reason I think the world population will continue to grow but then level off to about 10 billion people is that I believe that per capita income worldwide will grow. Empirically, as people's income grows, they have fewer children. We don't know exactly why that is true. Economists' knee-jerk theory is that higher per capita incomes imply a higher value placed on time, which implies a higher opportunity cost of raising children. Then, according to the law of demand, at a higher price fewer children are "demanded."

It turns out, though, that there are some problems with this straightforward way of explaining the strong empirical relationship between income and fertility. Laying out these problems would take me too far afield from the topic at hand,[2] but whatever the cause of the relationship, it is strong. As Larry Jones, Alice Schoonbroodt, and Michele Tertilt write, "A robust fact about fertility is that it is decreasing in income. This fact has been documented from a time-series point of view, across countries, and across individuals."[3]

The World Economy

I predict that the world economy in 2065, measured in real GDP, will be at least three times as large as it is today. That larger GDP will be due not mainly to higher population but to higher income per capita. The reason is that economic growth will be relatively high in China and India, where about 40 percent of the world's population lives, and in much of the rest of Asia, including Indonesia.

A simple arithmetic exercise would be useful here. For ease of calculation, assume that world GDP in 2065 is exactly three times its level in 2015 and that the world population is exactly 10 billion. Therefore, world population will have increased by about 39 percent. This means that GDP per capita must have increased by 216 percent. Over fifty years, that amounts to an annual average growth in real per capita income of 1.55 percent.

That growth is hefty but not spectacular, which is why I predict that world GDP will at least triple.

The main reason for my optimism is that it takes many barriers (high taxes, extreme regulation, etc.) to prevent such growth. I would not be surprised if there were more barriers to growth over the next fifty years than there are now. I would be very surprised, however, if those barriers prevented per capita GDP from growing by at least 1.55 percent annually.

The Chinese and U.S. Economies

According to the World Bank, China's GDP, measured in purchasing power parity, was $18.0 trillion in 2014, and U.S. GDP was $17.4 trillion.[4] In other words, China's economy is already the largest economy in the world. My prediction that U.S. GDP will be at least double its current level requires only that U.S. real GDP grow by an average of 1.4 percent per year. This is overall growth, not per capita growth. So assume that happens. For China's

GDP to be double U.S. GDP in 2065, China's annual growth rate of real GDP must average only 2.7 percent. Of course, U.S. GDP per capita would still be much higher than Chinese GDP per capita.

Moreover, this growth in real GDP in China, in the United States, and in the world will understate the growth of well-being. As innovations such as the Internet, Google, Facebook, and Yelp show, much of the value we currently get is from innovations whose output is priced at zero. Such value, therefore, does not show up in GDP data.

Why do I think it likely that China's economy will grow faster than the U.S. economy? Poorer economies that lag in technology but get basic institutions even approximately right can generally grow faster than more-mature economies. Of course, it is not clear that the Chinese government will get basic institutions even approximately right, but what is clear is that China is improving its basic institutions.

I hasten to add that I am not claiming that we need to worry about this likely event. In my view, we do not. I don't care if China's GDP grows by, say, 4 percent annually if ours grows by 2.5 percent annually. The vast majority of people in both countries will be much better off.

It is true that the Chinese government could use some of that added real GDP to strengthen its military. Indeed, that is likely. Unlike many people in Congress and many admirals I talk to in the U.S. Navy, however, I do not see this stronger Chinese military as a big threat to the United States. The Chinese government may threaten some of its neighbors. But as I said in a speech at a "boot camp" in Maryland for fifty-five newly chosen U.S. Navy admirals in October 2010, we have a major natural protection from the Chinese government: the Pacific Ocean. Although many of the admirals objected to my claim, all of their objections were about an increasingly powerful Chinese navy that would dominate that part of the world, not about a Chinese navy that might plausibly attack the United States or substantially disrupt its shipping lanes.

World Poverty

The World Bank's criterion for living in extreme poverty is having an income of $1.25 or less a day (in 2005 prices). In 1990, 1.91 billion people were in extreme poverty. In 2011, the number in extreme poverty had fallen to a little more than 1 billion, a drop by almost half.[5] I expect that by 2065 the number of people in extreme poverty will be less than half a billion owing to increased trade and internal growth only loosely connected to trade. It will not be due mainly to a massive increase in immigration to richer countries because the vast majority of governments of richer countries will not substantially relax their restrictions on immigration.

The Work Year

Many people believe that the increasing use of robots or increases in wealth or both will reduce the average number of hours that people work. I think this reduction will happen, but the effect will be modest. My prediction is that the average number of hours worked per year will fall by about 10 percent. People seem to like the extra wealth they can generate by working extra hours so they can buy the luxuries that suppliers are good at creating and supplying. Just as cell phones were a luxury twenty years ago and are now regarded as a necessity by most people in the wealthy and developing parts of the world, other luxuries will also become "necessities" over time.

Fuel and Mineral Prices

With more people in the world and more people with wealth, then, all other things being equal, there will be much higher demand for fuels and minerals. In the late 1980s and early 1990s, few people anticipated that India's and China's economies would grow as much as they did, putting pressure on prices. Such unanticipated increases in demand will cause increases in prices of fuels and minerals. In the longer run, however, the increases in prices will motivate people to search for more fuels and minerals, to produce more fuels and minerals from existing reservoirs and mines, and to figure out ways to conserve those fuels and minerals.[6]

Moreover, all other things are not equal. Jesse Ausubel[7] gives a fascinating, empirically backed exposition of the "dematerialization" of the United States. He points out, for example, that the cell phone has replaced maps, newspapers, cameras, CD players, and many other material-intensive items. He also notes that water use in the United States has stayed flat. This brief discussion does not do justice to his very optimistic look at the use of resources. That makes reasonable my estimate that a weighted average of mineral and fuel prices will be no more than 10 percent higher than what it is today.

U.S. Federal Government Spending

U.S. federal government spending, which is now about 21 percent of GDP, will go higher, but in 2065 it will not be higher than 25 percent of GDP. Although there are forces in the budget that look as if they will drive that number higher, the fact that federal revenues have averaged only about 18 percent of GDP for the past sixty-five years means that there will be great resistance to greater spending. What will happen to prevent government spending from going higher than this limit? Long before 2065, the federal government will default on its debt and will likely also scale back some of the major transfer programs such as Medicare and Social Security.[8] Although it is imaginable that tax revenues may rise to about 20 percent of GDP, revenues much higher than that are extremely unlikely. For that reason, 25 percent is a reasonable upper bound for government spending as a percentage of GDP, and it is likely to be lower than that.

U.S. Economic Freedom

According to James Gwartney, Robert Lawson, and Joshua Hall,[9] the level of economic freedom in the United States ties it with the United Kingdom for twelfth place out of 152 countries rated in 2013. U.S. economic freedom is likely to decline somewhat. Likely factors in the decline are increasing regulation of land use and housing supply, so that more of the United States has the same extreme regulations that coastal California, Oregon, and Washington have, as well as more extreme regulation of the workplace, making it harder for employers and employees to agree on flexible work arrangements. Also, some other countries' economic freedom is likely to increase. The U.S. economy will likely be at or slightly below twentieth place in 2065. Even if the U.S. level of economic freedom were to stay relatively constant, several economies outside the top twenty will likely displace established countries. And that would be alright.

If We Keep Our Ethical Wits, We Can See Over into a Great Enrichment

Art Carden and Deirdre N. McCloskey

For millions of years mankind lived just like the animals. Then something happened which unleashed the power of our imagination. We learned to talk and we learned to listen. Speech has allowed the communication of ideas, enabling human beings to work together to build the impossible. Mankind's greatest achievements have come by talking, and its greatest failures by not talking. It doesn't have to be like this. Our greatest hopes could become reality in the future. With the technology at our disposal, the possibilities are unbounded. All we need to do is make sure we keep talking.   —Stephen Hawking

THE DISCOURAGING RESULTS of Philip Tetlock's[1] inquiry into "expert political judgment," showing how poor in predictions the experts have been, leave us hesitant to make bold predictions, especially, as Yogi Berra once said, about the future. Yet, though prudence counsels preparation, the end is probably not nigh. Back up your hard drive, yes. Set up a Foundation[2] to hasten the galaxy's recovery from a chaotic interregnum, no.

Readers of Deirdre McCloskey's just-completed trilogy on the "Bourgeois Era"[3] will know that people are by historical standards astonishingly rich today because northwestern Europeans in early-modern times slowly adopted what she calls "the Bourgeois Deal." "Let me get rich with a trade-tested betterment in the first act, and in the third I will make *you* rich." People got richer not because of empire or investment or exploitation or institutional change, but because they changed their *ethics* and how they *talked* about betterment and competition and cooperation in trade-tested betterment. If people welcome betterment and competition and the amiable cooperation that both require, it turns out that they live longer and mightily prosper in body and soul. This deal worked wonders in Europe and its overseas extensions in the eighteenth and nineteenth centuries, surviving the clerisy's rebellion against bourgeois life after 1848 and even Europe's seventy-five-year suicide attempt from 1914 to 1989. It turned even places such as Hong Kong, Taiwan, South Korea, and Singapore from economic backwaters into some of the richest places on earth. The outcome was the Great Enrichment—disdained on both the socialist left and the conservative right: a thirty- to *one-hundred*-fold increase in the real incomes of the poorest among us since 1800. The Great Enrichment is nowadays causing in India and China humanity's largest exodus from poverty and now even in parts of sub-Saharan Africa, such as Botswana.

The cause of the bourgeois betterments was an economic liberation and a sociological dignifying of, say, a barber and wig maker of Bolton, son of a tailor, messing about with spinning machines, who died in 1792 as Sir Richard Arkwright, possessed of one of the largest bourgeois fortunes in England. The Industrial Revolution, and especially the Great Enrichment after it, came from the liberation of commoners from compelled service to a hereditary elite, such as the noble lord in the castle, or from compelled obedience to a state functionary, such as the economic planner in the capital. And it came from according honor to the formerly despised commoners of Bolton—or of Osaka or of Lake Wobegon—exercising their liberty to relocate a factory or invent airbrakes.

In view of the importance of how people talk, the new and even more egalitarian technology, belying the recent pessimism of Robert Gordon[4] and Tyler Cowen,[5] is talk on the Internet and the smartphone. As it gets cheaper and more ubiquitous, and as more minds once wasted in illiteracy and poverty join the Great Conversation, a bourgeois future looms. At a modest world growth rate of 3 percent per year, easily attainable with economic liberation and sociological dignifying in now tyrannical and hierarchical nations, the real per capita income in the world, now at about $33 per day, will quadruple by 2065, equal to U.S. income now. Some will get richer faster than others, yet everyone will be much, much richer. Even with widening inequality of wealth and income—we don't think it will happen, but let the Pikettys[6] have their say—there will be, as there has been in Germany and Japan since 1800, radically narrowing inequality of genuine comfort *in consumption*. Everyone will have indoor plumbing, the future cure for malaria, and university educations. Sub-Saharan Africa will produce the new Rumis and Mozarts and Einsteins.

In their book *Abundance* (2012) Peter Diamandis and Steven Kotler agree that the Great Enrichment is our future because of the billions of people who will over the next decade or so connect to the Internet. Our knowledge of human cognition is as yet of a meager and unsatisfactory kind. But it seems that the more we learn about neurodiversity—anticipated in Friedrich Hayek's theories of knowledge—and the more spaces online we create in which people of all types can thrive in market-tested betterment, the richer we get, literally and figuratively. Online communication is sweet for introverts, and the explosion of Internet communities and subcommunities and sub-subcommunities is sweet for people with unusual preferences. Who would have guessed that so many people love elevators? Carden wouldn't have before his seven-year-old son discovered on YouTube an online elevator community.

The Arab Spring demonstrated the power of social media and also, in the face of the government's monopoly of violence, its limits. Yet where previous generations had information sanitized by parents, politicians, preachers, and professors, Generations Y and Z can today with a few taps on a keyboard check anything against a virtually infinite array of sources. In the virtual world, anyone can self-author, self-create, self-politicize. Such self-authoring runs from the mundane (*Minecraft* videos) to the struggle for human rights— as exemplified by the My Stealthy Freedom Facebook page, which has an international following and is part of an Iranian woman's pushback against compulsory *hijab*. The Internet is even more of an equalizer than the printing of books or the democracy in church governance or the accidentally successful revolts and revolutions of the sixteenth through eighteenth century in northwestern Europe. And those events, after all, made the modern world.

Watch out, though. It is possible that the Internet will be used to bring back the *anti*bourgeois revolution that brought us nationalism and socialism, as well as (if you like those two) national socialism. Yet we are hopeful that more people will want to emulate Steve Jobs, Elon Musk, and Milton Friedman than Kaiser Wilhelm, Joseph Stalin, and Noam Chomsky. Rest well if the person on the plane next to you is reading on her Kindle *The Art of War*[7] to become a better manager in a company that specializes in pine straw installation. Lose sleep only if she is reading these books to lead a revolution against the commercial social order or to make actual, nonmetaphorical war in a program of populism of the left or right.

As Adam Smith said, "there is a great deal of ruin in a nation," and governments are not getting notably better at managing the people's money. The social-engineering notion that the government's responsibility is to internalize externalities and provide public goods is a mite better, to be sure, than the frankly extractive notions of earlier times, the Aristocratic Deal: "You honor me, an aristocrat by natural inequality, and give me the liberty to extract rents from you in the first act, and in the second and in all subsequent acts. I forbid you under penalty of death to seek competitive 'protection.' By the third act of the zero-sum drama, if you have behaved yourself and have pulled your forelock or made your curtsy as I ride by, I will not have slaughtered you." As economic historian Alexander Gerschenkron put it, reacting in 1971 to the claim by an economic theorist that feudal lords had offered "protection" to peasants, rather similar to the claims of internalizing externalities and providing public goods in recent times, "The possibility that the main, if not the only, danger against which the peasant very frequently was in need of protection was the very lord is not mentioned."[8] The government in most countries beyond northern Europe is "the very lord." Look at the unhappy results of the zero-sum worldview of politicians and pundits, quite sure from the right that foreigners will take our jobs or quite sure from the left that prosperity for some relies on poverty for the many.

Yet, along with Marx and Engels, we remain optimistic that there are enormous productive powers slumbering in the lap of social labor, led by the bourgeoisie, and that with a little luck even the government can't stop it. We are therefore, like Matt Ridley,[9] rational optimists. One would have expected the Stephen Hawking remark at the beginning of our essay to come from an address to an august nonprofit body such as the Royal Society. But it comes from a British Telecom commercial that aired in 1994 and was sampled in Pink Floyd's song "Keep Talking"—which was in turn part of an album that preceded one of the largest and most commercially successful tours of all time. Of such things—commerce and betterment, supported by praise for bourgeois virtues—we urge you: keep on talkin'.

6

The Coming of Peak
Gross Domestic Product?

Brink Lindsey

COULD ECONOMIC GROWTH come to an end in the next fifty years? Think whimper, not bang: A civilization-ending catastrophe isn't what I have in mind. Instead, the question is whether in the United States and other advanced countries growth as we have come to understand it could simply exhaust itself.

Speculation along these lines has become popular in the years since the Great Recession. Economist Robert Gordon[1] of Northwestern has argued provocatively that the best days of technological innovation are already behind us. Meanwhile, Lawrence Summers[2] of Harvard raises the prospect of "secular stagnation," in which a mismatch between savings and investment results in chronically anemic aggregate demand.

I want to explore another possibility. Let's assume that innovation continues to chug along and that opportunities for private investment suffice to keep secular stagnation at bay. Even so, I see a couple of scenarios in which growth as conventionally understood might come to an end. In both cases, the mechanism for growth's demise is the same: an ongoing decline in labor hours per capita. But whether this decline would be cause for celebration or sorrow depends on which workers reduce their labor hours and why.

When we talk about economic growth, we are typically referring to growth in the value of gross domestic product (GDP)—or, more precisely, to growth in real (i.e., inflation-adjusted) GDP per capita. To be sure, it is an imperfect measure. The calculation of GDP for any given year rests on a host of difficult methodological decisions; resolving those methodological issues in other, equally plausible ways would result in very different final figures. Just as daunting, if not more so, is the challenge of converting changes in nominal GDP from year to year into increases or decreases in real output. The price indexes used to make the conversion are increasingly sophisticated, but adjusting for quality improvements and the introduction of entirely new products ultimately comes down to educated guesswork.

Notwithstanding these difficulties, my judgment is that trends in real GDP do give us useful information about changes in the overall size of the "cash nexus"—that is, the market value of traded goods and services. Although some argue the point, I don't believe the measurement problems are getting worse over time; if anything, unmonetized welfare gains (what economists refer to as consumer surplus) were probably much bigger in the past. Consider, for example, the colossal improvements in well-being made possible by the rapid increase in life expectancy during the first half of the twentieth century. According to calculations by Kevin Murphy and Robert Topel of the University of Chicago, between 1900 and 1950 those gains alone were roughly equal to the value of all measured output.[3] I am quite confident that this unmeasured leap in material welfare dwarfs all the considerable thrills we get out of our smartphones these days. So if the numbers say that growth in GDP per capita is declining or has stopped, I think those numbers are telling us something important.

GDP per capita can be broken down into two basic components: labor hours per capita and output per worker-hour. Accordingly, if labor hours per capita start to decline, output per worker-hour must rise just to keep GDP from shrinking. Growth can occur only if the rise in labor productivity (output per worker-hour) outpaces the fall in labor hours.

The decline in labor hours per capita is no mere theoretical possibility. Between the first decade of the twentieth century and the early 1960s, annual hours worked per capita fell from more than 1,000 to less than 800 as the workweek shortened and young people exited the workforce to attend high school and, increasingly, college.[4] During this period, productivity growth was so robust, however, that real GDP per capita grew at roughly 2 percent a year in spite of the curtailment in work effort. From the mid-1960s to the end of the century, the combination of the Baby Boom and surging labor-force participation by women drove annual hours worked per capita back up again, ultimately exceeding 950 in 1999–2000. Productivity growth slowed markedly during this period, but the increase in work effort sufficed to keep overall real per capita output growth averaging 2 percent a year.

Since 2000, however, labor hours have resumed their decline. The Baby Boomers now are exiting the workforce, and women's as well as men's labor-force participation has been falling during the new century. With productivity growth also softening, leading forecasts for the upcoming decade or so suggest a drop-off in the long-term growth outlook from the historical norm of 2 percent annual growth to something in the range of 1 to 1.5 percent.[5] If labor hours continue on their downward trajectory, we will eventually reach the point of "peak GDP," after which the cash nexus will actually begin to contract.

There is absolutely no theoretical reason why this couldn't happen. Economists analyze the effect of economic growth on labor supply as a tug of war between the "income effect" (the rise in purchasing power caused by an increase in real wages) and the "substitution effect" (the change in relative prices caused by an increase in real wages). When their incomes rise, workers are faced with a choice: What do they buy with the extra money? Do they buy extra goods and services that they previously couldn't afford? Or do they, in effect, buy leisure instead, working less to consume the same product mix as before?

Economists generally think of leisure as a "normal good"—as income rises, people want more of it (as opposed to "inferior goods"—say, Ramen noodles or public transportation—consumption of which can be expected to decline as income rises). Accordingly, the income effect leads people to want to buy more leisure as their real wages rise. The substitution effect, however, cuts in the opposite direction: the relative price of leisure goes up with rising wages as the opportunity cost of extra leisure (i.e., the amount of money you give up by not working) is now higher than before. Which effect wins out? Economic theory is silent on the point. In any given case, the outcome turns on personal preferences.

Since the rise of the modern mass-production economy in the late nineteenth century, the historical pattern has been for American workers to split the difference. Over this period, a large share of real-wage gains has been consumed in the form of more leisure. According to economic historian Robert Fogel, when you include the imputed value of leisure as part of consumption, the share of total consumption devoted to leisure skyrocketed from 18 percent in 1875 to 68 percent by 1995.[6]

It should be noted that the move toward more leisure has doubtless been encouraged—sometimes deliberately, sometimes not—by public policy. Thus, Social Security has facilitated earlier retirement, and compulsory education and subsidies for schooling have worked to delay entry into the workplace. Meanwhile, numerous social programs offer benefits either not contingent on working (e.g., food stamps, housing assistance) or actually contingent on joblessness (e.g., Social Security Disability Insurance). These policies have thus accelerated the underlying trend.

Nevertheless, the explosion of new and improved goods and services over the past century and more has dissuaded Americans from taking it too easy. Although working life now starts later (because of more time in school) and ends relatively earlier (because of increased years spent in retirement), the forty-hour work week has remained the norm for more than seventy-five years. And since 1970 the percentage of employed men working more than fifty hours a week has actually risen considerably—a phenomenon concentrated among highly skilled top earners.[7]

But, as the saying goes, past performance is no guarantee of future results. Over the next half-century, the balance between the income effect and the substitution effect may shift decisively in favor of the former. In that event, economic growth as we currently conceive of it will come to an end.

Note that flat or declining GDP per capita need not mean the end of technological innovation or of new and improved products. Productivity growth can continue so long as labor hours decline as quickly or more quickly. Furthermore, well-being can keep improving in ways that don't show up in or are only partially registered by GDP statistics. The natural environment can be made cleaner and more beautiful; the privations and social exclusion of the poor can be mitigated; family and community life can become richer, deeper, and more satisfying; the boundaries of scientific knowledge can continue to be pushed back.

And huge, unmonetized welfare gains in the form of improved health and longevity remain possible. Imagine, for example, the advent of anti-aging therapies that become widely and inexpensively available. GDP per capita might shrink to the extent that the enormous and growing sums now spent on the diseases and complications of aging are no longer necessary, even as longevity gains that dwarf those of the twentieth century catapult well-being to new heights.

The great engine of human progress in the modern era—the division of labor through specialization and exchange—has been mediated largely within the cash nexus. But that won't necessarily be the case in the future. The new connectivity catalyzed by information technologies allows collaboration among strangers on a scale and at a level of sophistication that in the past was possible only when money changed hands. Think about open-source software or the free-culture movement or *Wikipedia*. As futurist Clay Shirky has noted, *Wikipedia* represents something like 100 million hours of human effort—compared to the 200 *billion* hours Americans spend cumulatively watching television every year.[8] Working with the enormous "cognitive surplus" of free time, as Shirky calls it, online tools have the potential to transform more and more of our leisure from passive consumption into active collaboration and creation.

This sunny picture of the possibilities of life after peak GDP rests on particular assumptions about why labor hours per capita continue falling. In this optimistic scenario, people "graduate" from the workforce into higher-value (in terms of well-being, not GDP) uses of their time. The relative attractions of working instrumentally for money recede as more and more of life's purchasable pleasures are attainable with less and less work effort; meanwhile, the possibilities for pursuing happiness outside the cash nexus proliferate as improved techniques for specialization and exchange without money changing hands boost the welfare "productivity" of leisure. Under these circumstances, the income effect of rising real wages gains sufficient ground against the substitution effect to extinguish per capita GDP growth—and people are better off as a result.

There is, however, a darker alternative scenario. Here, people don't graduate from the workforce; they instead drop out. Speculation is buzzing these days about the possibility of mass technological unemployment, as Moore's Law continues in operation and the capabilities of robots and other smart machines keep improving exponentially.[9] This prospect can be described as "capital-biased technological change": capital substitutes for workers across the skill spectrum, and the share of total national income going to labor falls over time.

Boys have been crying about this big bad wolf since the days of Ned Ludd. Perhaps the wolf is finally at the door, but the scenario I have in mind doesn't depend on anything so exotic and unprecedented. Rather, all that is needed is the continuation of the "skill-biased technological change" we have today, in which new technology (especially information technology) acts as a complement to high-skill workers (i.e., it increases their productivity and raises relative demand for them) but as a substitute for less-skilled laborers.

On the one hand, surely it is a good thing that economic life is growing less dependent on backbreaking manual labor and mindless clerical tedium. On the other, much of American society is failing to adapt to the new economic realities. Unstable families and a dysfunctional educational system produce large numbers of people with no valuable work skills and no real capacity to develop them. Meanwhile, automation and other technological progress keep whittling away at the best-paying mid-skill and low-skill jobs (because that's where the biggest cost savings are), forcing more workers to compete for the remaining less-attractive jobs they are qualified to do and therefore intensifying downward pressure on those wages.

Over time, then, more and more people with limited job skills find that the material welfare offered by life on the dole compares favorably to what they could earn in the labor market. And the increasing productivity of the high-skill sector, boosted by the same technological advances that reduce employment opportunities for the unskilled, allows society to carry a growing idle class at public expense. Accordingly, labor-force participation falls as discouraged low-skill workers drop out of the job market and live off public assistance.

This dynamic is already occurring. Wages for the less skilled have been stagnant or falling for decades now. According to calculations that paint a relatively sunny picture, wages for male high school dropouts fell 11 percent between 1973 and 2012, and those for high school grads rose only 4 percent. The most widely cited statistics, meanwhile, are even bleaker.[10] (However, it should be noted that these figures omit benefits such as health insurance, which have increased as a percentage of total compensation over time.) And although labor-force participation for all men has been falling, the drop has been concentrated among the less skilled. Between 1969 and 1999, as labor-force participation overall was reaching its historic high, the participation rate for "prime-age" (twenty-five- to fifty-four-year-old) white males with college degrees inched down from 98 to 96 percent, and the rate for black prime-age college grads dipped from 94 to 92 percent. The numbers for prime-age male high school dropouts look very different: the participation rate for whites fell from 95 to 83 percent, and for blacks it dropped from 91 to 61 percent.[11] As work effort falls, dependency rises. Thus, the percentage of adults ages twenty-five to sixty-four receiving benefits from Social Security Disability Insurance has shot up from 2.3 percent in 1989 to 5.0 percent in 2013.[12]

Here, then, we are not talking about rising real wages that lead more and more people to opt for self-financed leisure. Here we are talking about flat or even declining real wages that increase the relative appeal of taxpayer-financed joblessness. This dynamic doesn't involve the interplay of income effect and substitution effect; the relevant economic concept here is the "reservation wage," the minimum pay that will motivate a worker to take a job. If market wages for the unskilled fall or the level of public support rises, more and more workers will find that their market value is lower than their reservation wage, and so they will exit the labor market accordingly.

In this scenario, greater leisure doesn't lead to improved well-being. After all, the same cognitive, interpersonal, and motivational skills needed for success in the workplace are equally necessary for "productive" leisure. Labor-force dropouts who lack the skills for workplace success are therefore unlikely to put their free time to good use. Instead of enjoying creative, productive, and often highly organized leisure, discouraged workers are much more likely to fall into an inescapable trap of idleness, dissipation, disconnection, and anomie. Time-use studies show that the jobless don't use much of their extra free time to better themselves or to serve their communities. Instead, most of that extra time is consumed sleeping longer and watching a lot more TV.[13]

Again, none of this is hypothetical: it is happening right now. All it takes is extrapolation to get to the end of economic growth. If current trends continue, the idle class could grow large enough that labor hours per capita no longer suffice to keep real GDP per capita on an upward path.

So will either of these growth-ending scenarios actually come to pass? For what it's worth, my bet is no. As to the first option, I expect the hit parade of new and improved commercial products to continue with sufficient allure that workers will be enticed to maintain their labor hours at growth-consistent levels. As to the second option, I suspect that political constraints on providing public assistance to people who don't work will be binding enough to prevent expansion of the idle class from swallowing economic growth.

Nonetheless, I think it's instructive to ponder these possibilities. Both scenarios, after all, are spun from trends clearly visible today. It is useful, then, to project what the world would look like if these trends were to continue and accelerate. What becomes apparent, especially from the juxtaposition of the two possible futures, is that individual human flourishing—not rising GDP per capita—ought to be the ultimate object of our concern. Although the two have been linked since the Industrial Revolution, they need not always remain so. In our individual lives, when making decisions about what we now call work/life balance, we frequently make choices that further our individual welfare but reduce GDP per capita. We should be alert to the possibility that our collective choices might someday have the same effect.

7

Why Software Really Will Eat the World—and Whether We Should Worry

Russell D. Roberts

PREDICTING THE FUTURE of the economy is a fool's game. Go back fifty or one hundred years and imagine trying to see where we are now. Our Internet-connected world, with its consequences for business and entertainment, was unimaginable even twenty-five years ago, so talking about what comes next demands humility. What I will try to do here is not predict the future but rather suggest what trends and processes may prove important in the coming decades and what might interrupt those trends along the way.

Some economists—Robert Gordon,[1] for example—have suggested that the rate of productivity growth has slowed significantly, so we should expect low growth rates for some time looking forward. I have a different perspective. Much of the improvement in the quality of our daily lives cannot be captured with traditional methods of data collection using standard economic variables such as gross domestic product. The explosion in low-cost entertainment via the Internet, for example, has been extraordinary, and much of that pleasure and delight is scarcely monetized, if at all.

And I think the best is yet to come as the digital revolution, ubiquitous smartphones, and Moore's Law continue to change our lives. Personalized medicine, online education, and transportation are just a few important areas where I think technology is potentially transformative. Let's look at each of these areas briefly.

In medicine, you can use your iPhone to take a picture of the inside of your child's ear, upload it to the Cloud, and have a doctor tell you whether your child has an ear infection. You can monitor whether your elderly parents are taking their medication from a thousand miles away. A single drop of blood can now be used for dozens of tests at lower prices than those charged by the current

43

laboratory duopoly, Quest and Laboratory Corporation of America. You can consult with a doctor online for general health issues. You can even bring a doctor to your house, Uber style.

Khan Academy, Udacity, Coursera, and EdX are beginning to change the world of education. They offer low-cost, high-quality pedagogy. Many problems remain with testing, certification, and classroom interaction, but we are at the very beginning of this revolution. Much trial and error are under way, and the best techniques will survive and thrive.

In transportation, the driverless car and truck will save thousands of lives each year, potentially making human driving obsolete, reducing the necessary width of city streets, ending the need for each house to store a car either in the driveway or the garage, and giving older people who struggle with driving a new sense of freedom.

All of these digitally driven improvements are examples of what entrepreneur and venture capitalist Marc Andreessen calls "software eating the world."[2] Software is transforming existing industries in quantum leaps rather than through incremental changes.

If driverless cars and trucks come to be, they don't just reduce the number of taxi drivers and truck drivers. They eliminate an entire industry. If robots can do surgery with little or no human involvement, the demand for human doctors falls dramatically. If I can learn everything I want to know online, the best teachers will teach millions, and the need for teachers will be a tiny fraction of what it is now.

Are these reductions in employment (driven by immense productivity) a feature or a bug? Throughout human history, these kinds of changes created an ever-growing prosperity. Getting more from less is the standard way technology has led to higher living standards in the past. When economies can produce more output with fewer inputs, that frees up those inputs to create other things. So the immense improvements in agricultural productivity over the past century freed up workers who once would have been farmers to do other things instead. We gained cheaper food and more of many other things—airplanes, cars, smartphones, movies enhanced with computer-generated imagery, healthcare, and so on. If 40 percent of the workforce had to work in agriculture today as they did in 1900, we wouldn't have all of those new innovations. We wouldn't be able to spare the people to think of them, create them, and produce them.

But if software eats the world, will new opportunities be created to take advantage of the skills of displaced workers? What will all the people driving taxis and trucks do if driverless cars and trucks become common? Some economists worry that virtually every activity will be more cheaply produced or created by smart machines than by people.

Activities that will remain are conceiving and creating more clever or more useful machines. But the ability to do this is scarce. What will the rest of the workforce do?

I remain guardedly optimistic. Just as it is hard to guess or predict what humans will be good for in a smart-machine age, it is hard to imagine that we will be unable to come up with new activities that are also productive. Another worry is that when such activities that we cannot imagine today do indeed become available, the wages for the lowest-skilled workers will be distressingly low. Perhaps. But those wages will go a long way in a world where software is eating the world.

The key characteristic of software is that additional copies are nearly free. That means we don't need more and more workers to produce the additional copies of a software program's output in the way we need more and more workers to create more traditional brick-and-mortar products. This reality cuts both ways for the average worker. They may not be needed to produce those extra copies, but those extra copies will be very inexpensive, so even seemingly low wages will allow for a very high standard of living.

The biggest problem may be that a large proportion of humanity will be able to live very well without having to do much work. The challenge we will face will not be physical scarcity but spiritual scarcity. Many of us get meaning from our work. What will life be like if many of us hardly have to work at all? I don't know the answer other than to point out that this is a better problem to have than the challenges of a world where a billion people or more live at the edge of subsistence.

The other important observation to make is that these transformative trends are threatened by regulatory or other types of barriers. Uber drivers face arrest or being forced to work in the same way that taxi drivers do. Universities (encouraged by faculty members) are uneasy with accepting online courses because they correctly see them as a threat to many faculty members' livelihood. Existing medical companies are fighting the medical innovators. All of these changes must overcome psychological barriers, too.

Right now, in 2015, the regulatory challenges look formidable. But it is hard to imagine that existing competitors will be able to stop changes that make consumers' lives mainly better. Improvements happen. They happen even when existing competitors flex their political muscle to stop those improvements. They may be slowed down. In America, they are almost never stopped.

Government does many stupid and wasteful things, but that doesn't stop creative, driven people from continuing to innovate. It doesn't stop my kids from getting a decent education. But it stops other kids who are growing up in more challenging circumstances from participating in the parts of the economy that remain dynamic. The minimum wage and our lousy public schools don't hurt my kids. But they hurt millions of others. I don't know if the digital revolution will weaken the public-school monopoly or force public schools to do a better job. But if we want a future where all people have a decent chance to flourish, introducing a little more competition into schools and labor markets would go a long way.

8

The U.S. Economy

The New Normal and an Unsustainable Future

Benjamin Powell and Taylor Leland Smith

IT IS WITH some trepidation that we contribute to a symposium on the future of the economy. The future is inherently unknowable. Although the laws of economics are universal, the institutional environments within which they operate dictate economic outcomes. Thus, any prediction about the future is ultimately a prediction about institutional evolution. Formal institutions are often shaped by political decisions, and those political decisions are shaped by broader cultural forces. We do not have a comparative advantage in forecasting political or cultural evolution.

Our goal here is more modest. First, we outline where the economy is today and why it is behaving as it is. Next, we project current economic policy into the future and find it unsustainable. Thus, some evolution of policy and institutions is inevitable. Our final section speculates on the forms that evolution might take.

The New Normal

The U.S. recession officially ended in June 2009.[1] Yet since the end of the recession, annual growth in gross domestic product (GDP) has averaged only 2.2 percent.[2] Meanwhile, unemployment has averaged a little more than 8 percent, and even this percentage understates the problem because many are underemployed or have dropped out of the labor force altogether.[3]

The working-age population of the United States has grown by roughly 51 million people since 1994, yet we have added only 21 million jobs. The remaining 30 million people either have left the workforce altogether or are

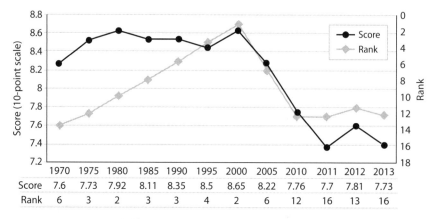

	1970	1975	1980	1985	1990	1995	2000	2005	2010	2011	2012	2013
Score	7.6	7.73	7.92	8.11	8.35	8.5	8.65	8.22	7.76	7.7	7.81	7.73
Rank	6	3	2	3	3	4	2	6	12	16	13	16

Source: Data compiled from Gwartney, Lawson, and Hall 2015.

Figure 1. United States, Economic Freedom of the World Rank and Score, 1970–2013

categorized as "underemployed," "discouraged," or "marginally attached to the work force."[4]

This sluggish economy contrasts sharply with U.S. economic performance in the twenty years prior to the recession. During that time, the economy expanded by 75 percent, growing at a real annualized rate of 3.0 percent.[5] Over the same period, roughly 63 percent of the U.S. labor force was employed. Since the end of the recession, that number has dropped to 59 percent.[6]

The U.S. economy's poor performance is no longer related to our most recent business cycle. It instead reflects the type of long-run growth that can be expected due to our decreased economic freedoms. The *Economic Freedom of the World Annual Report* is the best measure of economic freedom available. It measures thirty-one variables across five broad categories: size of government; property rights; sound money; freedom to trade internationally; and regulation of credit, labor, and business.[7]

The United States ranked in the top four in the world in every year economic freedom was measured between 1970 and 2000 (figure 1). But since the year 2000 U.S. economic freedom has been on the decline. The United States fell from second in 2000 to a low of sixteenth in 2011, thirteenth in 2012, and then sixteenth again in 2013, and its rating (out of ten) fell from 8.65

in 2000 to 7.73 in 2013. The decline in freedom has been almost across the board.[8] Probably most troubling has been the growth of the size of the U.S. government and the perceived decrease in the security of our property rights. Adjusting for inflation, the U.S. government spends 40 percent more today than it did in 2000.[9] As the next section outlines, this increased spending is expected to accelerate to unsustainable levels in the coming years.

To measure security of property rights, the index relies on a number of surveys in the *International Country Risk Guide*, the *Global Competitiveness Report*, and the World Bank's *Doing Business* project in assessing how secure property rights are here.[10] The U.S. score for this variable has decreased from 9.2 to 7.0 since 2000. No single "smoking gun" can be pointed to as the reason for the decrease in perceived security of property rights. Possible contributing factors might include the Supreme Court's *Kelo* decision[11] that eminent domain can be used for economic development; the increasing seizure by police of personal property of individuals suspected of being involved in the drug trade (without a court verdict or even charges being filed); and the wholesale rewriting of contracts by the government during the bailouts of 2008.[12]

A large literature shows that economic freedom is associated with higher incomes, faster economic growth, longer life expectancies, and most other measures of well-being that people generally care about.[13] Using one estimate[14] of how economic freedom impacts growth rates, we can estimate that the 0.92 drop in the Economic Freedom Index score for the United States since 2000 should be expected to generate annual growth rates that are 0.736 percentage points lower than they were prior to our decline in economic freedom. This means that a significant portion of our sluggish growth can be attributed to our lower level of economic freedom, but even this correlation understates the impact our decreased freedom can have on growth because changes in economic freedom, regardless of absolute level of freedom, have also been shown to be important for economic growth. So the fact that our decline to a new lower level of freedom is recent is also likely contributing to slower growth. In short, the U.S. economy's sluggish growth is our new normal rather than a product of a business cycle.

Absent a change in the U.S. institutional environment, the future of the U.S. economy looks—based on our deteriorated economic freedom—much like the slow-growth economy we have today. However, due to the impending explosion in entitlement obligations, it is very unlikely that our current environment of economic freedom will be stable.

An Unsustainable Future

Increased government spending played a role in decreasing economic freedom in the United States over the past dozen years. However, that growth in spending pales in comparison to the growth in government spending that would be required for existing government policies to continue in the future.

The U.S. government's official debt of $18.3 trillion amounts today to roughly 103 percent of GDP. Approximately 73 percent of the federal debt is held by the public. According to the U.S. Congressional Budget Office,[15] this publicly held debt is expected to grow to between 92 percent and 135 percent of GDP by 2039. By 2089, it is expected to balloon to 225 percent of GDP. As the European debt crisis has shown, these debt levels are wholly unsustainable.[16] Forecasted unfunded liabilities in the Social Security and Medicare programs are an even larger problem than official debt forecasts. The "fiscal gap" is an estimate of differences between what these programs have promised to pay out and their forecast revenue. According to Laurence Kotlikoff, who helped to develop generational accounting to measure these unfunded liabilities, "The size of the U.S. fiscal gap—$210 trillion—is massive. It's 16 times larger than official U.S. debt, which indicates precisely how useless official debt is for understanding our nation's true fiscal position."[17] Other estimates indicate a gap between $54.4 trillion and $91.4 trillion.[18] Although these estimates vary widely, the unfunded liabilities even at the bottom of the range dwarf the official government debt by orders of magnitude.

The current fiscal trajectory is unsustainable. Given the U.S. decline in economic freedom, robust economic growth is unlikely to occur and ease these burdens. Programs such as Social Security rely on getting more young workers in to pay the benefits of the old. Current demographic trends indicate that U.S. birthrates will not help, and it seems politically unlikely that the U.S. government will significantly increase immigration quotas (and even if they did, most dynamic and generational estimates of the net fiscal impact of immigrants are clustered around zero).[19] Thus, a change in fiscal policy is necessary.

Kotlikoff estimates that to remain solvent in the future, "[w]e need to either reduce the time path of government expenditures by 10.5 percent of GDP or raise the time path of government revenues by 10.5 percent of GDP. Alternatively, we can enact a combination of spending cuts and tax increases that amount to 10.5 percent of annual GDP. This adjustment needs to begin immediately and continue forever."[20] Is a policy change of this magnitude likely?

Which Way Forward?

To say that current U.S. fiscal policy is unsustainable is only to say that it must change. Predicting precisely how and when it will change is much less a matter of economic science. Nevertheless, we can speculate on how likely the necessary reforms are to occur and what the consequences will be if they do not.

It is first worth noting the staggering size of the adjustment in fiscal policy that is necessary. Federal tax revenue as a percentage of GDP has been a little lower than and occasionally bumped up against the 20 percent level since the end of World War II, and it peaked briefly at 22 percent during the war.[21] Permanently increasing taxes by 10.5 percent of GDP seems highly unlikely. Even splitting the burden and increasing taxes as a percentage of GDP by 5.25 percent would require the political support that was achieved only during World War II for a brief time period. It seems highly unlikely, at least absent a crisis occurring, that the American voters will support a tax increase of anything close to the magnitude necessary to stave off a fiscal collapse.

Budget cuts and cuts to promised entitlements of any magnitude large enough to significantly close the fiscal gap also seem unlikely. The budget sequestration in 2013 cut spending authority by $85 billion for that fiscal year[22] and is estimated to cut spending by a total of $1.2 trillion over an eight-year period.[23] This relatively trivial spending cut, which exempted Social Security, was deemed "austerity" in the popular press and vigorously objected to by its political opponents. If such a trivial spending cut generates that reaction, it is a strong indication that the type of cuts necessary to seriously address the fiscal gap are politically impossible, even if coupled with tax increases.

If increased growth and migration are unlikely to save the United States from a fiscal crisis, and the political will doesn't exist to cut spending or increase taxes enough in order to avert a fiscal crisis, then signs point in the direction of a fiscal crisis in the future. Although impossible to predict the timing precisely, the crisis will come before all of the bills are due. Once debt holders begin realizing that there is no way the U.S. government will be able to meet all of its debt and entitlement obligations and start requiring greater risk premiums on government bonds, the crisis will come on quite quickly, as it did in Greece.

It is beyond the scope of this brief essay to predict how such a fiscal crisis might play out. Would radical spending cuts or tax increases become politically possible in the midst of a fiscal meltdown? In that situation, would Medicare or Social Security be significantly cut or even abolished? Would foreign governments intervene to partially bail out the United States? Would the government be forced to default on or even repudiate its debt?[24] Would it choose to go the way of Zimbabwe and hyperinflate?

If such a fiscal crisis comes about, we hope that it will lead to a reassessment of the role government plays in the economy, a reassessment that would make the type of reductions in the size and scope of government that are not politically possible today. As Milton Friedman observed more than fifty years ago, "Only a crisis produces real change. . . . This, I believe, is our basic function: to develop alternatives to existing policies, to keep them alive and available until the politically impossible becomes the politically inevitable."[25] The advocates of laissez-faire need to continue to develop the intellectual alternatives to welfare statism and articulate them to a broad audience. Perhaps, just perhaps, once the folly of the unsustainable welfare state is revealed, people will embrace the market and civil society alternatives.[26]

9

Life Is a Battlefield

Janet A. Schwartz and Dan Ariely

"SET FIRE TO YOUR HAIR/Poke a stick at a grizzly bear." So begins "Dumb Ways to Die," one of the most popular public-service announcements of all time, where colorful, singing blobs warn viewers about the most foolish ways to end their lives. Created by McCann, an American advertising agency, the animated ad was launched in November 2012 to reduce railway accidents caused by reckless passenger behavior on Metro Trains Melbourne. Just forty-eight hours after the video's release, the song reached number six in the singer-songwriter category on the iTunes charts globally. Today, the catchy tune has acquired more than 100 million views on YouTube:

> Set fire to your hair
> Poke a stick at a grizzly bear
> Eat medicine that's out of date
> Use your private parts as piranha bait

Chorus: Dumb ways to die
> So many dumb ways to die
> Dumb ways to die
> So many dumb ways to die

> Get your toast out with a fork
> Do your own electrical work
> Teach yourself how to fly
> Eat a two-week-old unrefrigerated pie

(Chorus)

Invite a psycho-killer inside
Scratch a drug dealer's brand new ride
Take your helmet off in outer space
Use your clothes dryer as a hiding place

(Chorus)

Keep a rattlesnake as a pet
Sell both your kidneys on the Internet
Eat a tube of superglue
I wonder, what this red button will do?

(Chorus)

Dress up like a moose during hunting season
Disturb a nest of wasps for no good reason
Stand on the edge of a train station platform
Drive around the boom gates at a level crossing

Run across the tracks between the platforms
They may not rhyme but they're quite possibly
The dumbest ways to die
So many dumb ways to die die die die die die die die die[1]

"Dumb Ways to Die" is a very catchy song, so unless you want to keep on singing it in your mind for the rest of the day, don't go to YouTube, don't type "Dumb Ways to Die," and don't watch it.

Although the tune is very catchy, and although running "across the tracks between the platforms" is undoubtedly a dumb move, we suspect that the real dumb ways to die are much more mundane and much less spectacular. And even worse, it might be the case that the really dumb ways to die are not the rare occurrences where we mistakenly run into trouble—they are the result of technologies that we deliberately create without thinking too much about their potential downside. Take texting, for example, and then combine it with walking or driving. . . .

Texting while driving is clearly a dangerous, reckless, and stupid thing to do, but it is also a useful metaphor to help us think about some of the ways in which we misbehave—ways that are inconsistent with our long-term interests.

Overeating, undersaving, overborrowing, and underexercising are just a few of the short-sighted behaviors we're often guilty of. The list goes on and on. The rising problem is that our ability to act in our long-term interest is only getting more and more difficult! Why? Because our world has become more hostile to our ability to make decisions. It is a world in which everyone wants something from us—our money, our attention, our time—and they're armed not with guns but with our vices. Adding to the challenges is the sad fact that the way we design the world around us does not help us fight temptation and think long term. In fact, if an alien were to observe the way we design the world, the only sensible conclusion he could come to is that human beings are determined to create more and more temptations that make us think more and more myopically and make more and more mistakes. Think about it: Will the next version of the donut (donut 2.0) be more tempting or less tempting? Will the next version of the smartphone get us to check it more or less throughout the day? And will the next version of Facebook tempt us to update our status more or less frequently?

One of the most important lessons from the social and behavioral sciences over the past few decades is that our surroundings influence our behavior to a much larger degree than we realize. Of course, some people and institutions do care about our long-term interests—our spouses and families, perhaps our religious organizations, or maybe even Medicare and life insurance companies—but most of these entities are not part of our moment-to-moment environment. The environment we live in is made up largely of entities that want us to be impulsive and live in the right here, right now. Facebook updates, Google alerts, and Gilt flash sales are their ammunition; and by making us feel good in the moment, these entities make us focus on what's good for them in the short term instead of what's good for us in the long term. In essence, our behavior is shaped by people who bank on how easily we will give in to temptation.

We may think that now that we know these commercial interests are after us, our time, our money, and our attention, there's something we can do about it. After all, we often believe ourselves to be reasonable and rational beings. So we just have to have the right information to make good decisions, and we will immediately make the right decisions. We eat too much? Just provide calorie information, and all will be well. We don't save enough? Just start using a retirement calculator and watch our savings grow. Texting while driving? Just tell everyone how dangerous it is. Kids drop out of school. Doctors don't wash their hands before checking their patients. Let's just explain to the kids why they should stay in school and tell the doctors why they should wash their hands. Sadly, life is not that simple, and most of the problems we have in modern life are not due to lack of information, which explains why our repeated attempts to improve behavior by providing additional information often do so little to make things better.

What Next?

If the problems of self-control are indeed central to our long-term well-being as individuals and as a society, then we must think of countermeasures to offset the constant and increasing pressure to live in the moment. If information is good at changing attitudes and intentions but isn't good at changing behavior, what can we do? What are the ways in which we can make the environment better so that we behave in healthier, wealthier, and safer ways? If we believe (and not all of us do) that people are fallible and can be overtly tempted or even gently misguided into doing what others want, then we have to think about paternalism. Why are we so averse to such paternalism?

In some cases, we see the value in it, especially when we think of ways in which human beings make physical mistakes. Let's return to driving—accidents and collisions are often caused by human error such as distractions and drowsiness. As a society, we recognize that we aren't perfect, and so we get better and better at designing roads with reflectors, guardrails, and built-in rumble strips that jolt us back into our lane. We recognize that these measures don't solve all the problems, so we go even one step further to make cars that sound an alarm or even take control of the car for you if you're drifting lanes or are about to collide with the car in front of you. Designing roads and cars that accommodate our inevitable mistakes seems sensible; after all, we are human, and we can't be perfect all the time. However, designing fast-food restaurants, malls, and credit cards to intentionally prevent (rather than exploit) our unavoidable mistakes feels wrong.

One problem with a paternalistic approach to engineering environments is our discomfort with the idea of someone trying to restrict our free will—that someone else is deciding what's best for us and forcing us to go along even if we disagree. The problem is not that we don't recognize that a terrible tension exists in the space between what we feel like doing in the moment and how we ought to behave for the long term, but that it is a deeply personal space. Who possibly has the right to tell us how many donuts is enough or whether a soda is too big? If we ate too many donuts this time, it's easy to trick ourselves into thinking that in the future we won't do it again. In the future, we have perfect information and with it perfect self control. And eating too many donuts is certainly not the same as mindlessly or mistakenly wandering into the next lane of traffic. Or is it? How do we balance our personal freedom and desire to enjoy life's pleasures in moderation with our inability to moderate?

Society offers both soft and hard approaches to being paternalistic. Paternalistic policies in their strictest form decide what is best for us regardless of whether we agree. Seatbelt and anti-texting laws are good examples. Even if you think you won't get in an accident, you risk a steep fine if you get caught unbuckled or reminding your beloved it's his or her turn to pick up the milk. And even though car crashes may be rare, imagining them is very vivid—you can see the wreckage and the injuries as a direct result of one bad decision. This ability to imagine the worst makes paternalism more tolerable; we can see how everyone benefits from it, even if some disagree. But what about eating too many donuts or splurging on a new pair of jeans? Here the bad effects accumulate little by little, and it is harder to connect any one instance of over-indulgence or poor self-control to a specific poor health or financial outcome. This lack of a clear connection makes restrictive policies less tolerable.

Softer paternalistic approaches can help align our good intentions with our desire to behave well, but they also give us great flexibility. They provide us with easy ways to act on the information in the form of calorie labels, retirement savings calculators, or credit-card interest disclosures. They balance our social obligation to ensure good decision making and the preservation of our individual free will. Softer approaches take the position that we know in principle what's in our best interest and that once we are properly informed and guided, our behavior will fall in line. If we want to be wealthy in retirement, we know that saving is better than buying donuts, ringtones, or extra video game lives right now. But how often does knowing this really mean that we will put away money for the rent and food and electricity we will be using thirty years from now? This probably doesn't happen very often because our good intentions face fierce competition from the world around us—from the entities who want our money or time or attention right now, not in the future. And they are very good at getting it, in part because they create the physical and virtual environments in which we live, in part because they know precisely how to tempt us, and in part because we don't fully understand or acknowledge some of the most basic aspects of our nature.

Somewhere in between soft and hard paternalism is a more libertarian approach. This approach recognizes that big obstacles block our good intentions from becoming actual behaviors, but it stops short of imposing inflexible restrictions or penalties. In the libertarian approach, instead of giving people lots of information about retirement savings and letting them decide on the right mutual fund, we can automatically put them into a good mutual fund that performs well for most people and then let them opt out if they want something different. Here we can tolerate a little paternalism in choosing what that default is because most people both wish they were better at saving for retirement and tend to stick to the default option. If people are further unsure of how much to save, we can suggest a default amount, say 7 percent, and let them adjust according to their needs. Again, because most people stick to the default, the social planner can assume that 7 percent is a reasonably good estimate of the savings rate moving forward. The social planner can take further steps toward the paternalistic approach by making it hard but not impossible to dip into that money if there's a real emergency. Of course, these one-time decisions may be challenging to set up at first, but they are easy to keep going once they are in place—precisely because they capitalize on our tendency to do nothing. The real question is, What can we do about the situations that require ongoing effort and long-term self-control? Eating well, exercising, driving safely, avoiding distractions and the temptation to overspend are all things that are good for us in the long term but difficult to achieve in any one moment, let alone the string of moments that make up daily life.

If we stop for a minute to think about the future—where it will likely be harder and harder to resist temptation—a central question in designing what that future environment should look like must incorporate a framework for necessary paternalism. How much freedom should people have given what we know about how they really behave as opposed to the idealized version of how they ought to behave? We are quick to develop strategies for making cars and roads safer because we know that even careful, attentive drivers can make mistakes. We can acknowledge that failures to regulate behavior can be disastrous, so there are fines and penalties for not wearing seatbelts and for texting or drinking while driving. But we really have to think about whether it should remain OK to sell six-hundred-calorie sodas to our increasingly overweight children or to continue to give credit to people who can't afford to pay back their loans or save for retirement. Once we can acknowledge that self-control failures are inevitable and that we are too optimistic about our ability to overcome them in the future, we can design environments that help us work toward our own goals rather than toward someone else's. Until then, corporations and other commercial interests who think it's best for us to live only in the moment and be unprepared for the future will determine the environment in which we live and, by extension, our behavior.

10

The Uber-All Economy of the Future

J. Walker Smith

THE POSTER CHILD for the economy of the future is Uber, the much ballyhooed (and much booed) on-demand mobile service for transportation. It's more than transportation, though. Every nook and cranny of the consumer economy is being "Uberized" by a business model that twins personal services with technology. Not only does this business model fit the competitive opportunities of today's marketplace, but it also dovetails seamlessly with the larger dynamics shaping tomorrow's marketplace. What's ahead is a shift in the dominant business model, one in which all consumer goods will be available as a service and all consumer services will be available on demand. This is the Uber-All Economy of the future.

Anticipating the future in this way is a bottom-up view of change. The usual line-up of macrolevel shifts in productivity-enhancing technologies and labor-force demographics will be critical, of course, but the most important dynamic is happening at the level of the firm. Companies will make money in different ways, and this will cascade through the economy. Changes in technology and in the labor force are setting the stage for this transformation not by enabling companies to do something old in new ways but by forcing companies to do something entirely new.

The success of Uber and of companies with an Uber-like business model is particularly noteworthy in the context of a global economy struggling with slow growth. Technology is unlocking these opportunities. In particular, mobile applications are enabling start-ups to aggregate sufficient demand to support this new business model, often by capturing unrealized value from assets these start-ups do not own. But even when new infrastructure is required, needed investments are lower, which reduces start-up costs and time to market.

Equally important, technology is closing the gap between decisions made by consumers and the satisfaction of those choices. Speed has always been important, but immediacy will be the ante going forward. Machines are better at immediacy than people, not to mention more productive for both routine and abstract tasks. The displacement of people by machines will put the labor force under increasing pressure, with a shrinkage of jobs in many sectors and a growth of jobs assured only in personal services and technology, a duality of future employment that matches the twin elements central to the Uber-All business model.

Every Category

No business category will be unaffected by companies operating with an Uber-like, on-demand business model. For illustrative purposes, consider a well-established category such as laundry detergent. The competitive set for laundry detergents is no longer just the traditional products on a grocery store shelf but also includes companies such as FlyCleaners, Washio, Rinse and Dryv in the United States, Laundrapp in the United Kingdom, and Edaixi in China, all of which operate through an on-demand mobile app. With the click of a button, consumers get their laundry picked up and returned right away, clean and ready to wear. Obviously, such a service is not directly substitutable with a bottle of liquid laundry detergent, but it is a direct substitute for the same benefit—clean clothes when needed.

Every benefit can be addressed in many ways by solutions of many forms, and that is both the threat and the opportunity posed by the Uber-All Economy. Net benefits are all that matter to consumers. The Uber-All Economy is reshaping how benefits are delivered, thereby reframing what consumers expect and want.

Even more broadly, if the need for clean clothes is better met through an on-demand mobile service, then it's not just laundry detergent that's no longer needed but also at-home washers and dryers, and if there is no need for washers and dryers, then there's no need for a laundry room in the home either. Something similar is true for every category, such as meal-delivery services affecting kitchens and pantries or transportation services affecting cars and garages. As such trade-offs get sorted out in household budgets, the superior net value of on-demand mobile services will become more apparent, and as it does, the diffusion of the Uber-All business model will gather momentum.

Business Model

Two elements are critical to the Uber-All business model. The first is a personal service. Uber itself is a personal service of drivers. Washio or Fly-Cleaners is a personal service for cleaning clothes. But consumer goods are also affected because Uber-All companies want to substitute their personal services for these goods.

The concept at work here is conversion—converting goods into services and converting underleveraged service assets into more valuable ones. For Uber, idle car-and-driver assets are converted from nonuse to use. Consumer goods must add a service or find a service within which to get embedded. Services need to innovate what they do to stay ahead of the broader conversion of value into something tied to a service in every category.

The second element of the Uber-All business model is on-demand availability anywhere, anytime. Technology makes this possible. To date, mobile apps have been central to this model, but on-demand availability is fundamentally about fulfillment in whatever way is fastest. The specific technologies are sure to evolve.

One important consequence of on-demand availability is tiered pricing tied to occasions. Many on-demand mobile services charge a premium today, but this is not the essence of on-demand pricing, and premium pricing will come down as competition and scale grow. The essence is pay-as-you-go pricing.

The Uber-All business model is pricing for usage rather than pricing for ownership or accumulation. In contrast, generally speaking, pricing today is based on accumulation, not on usage or demand in the moment. Stocking up or subscribing or collecting entail pricing by accumulation, not pricing by usage.

With the Uber-All on-demand business model, a brand sells by the slice—no more than a consumer needs in that moment. This has two key implications. First, it erodes the need for ownership. Access replaces ownership at the center of consumers' aspirational mindset. In addition, access instead of ownership means a shift toward consumers paying only the marginal cost of production, which in turn leaves less room for mark-ups by producers and retailers.

Second, the priority in pricing shifts from targeting people to targeting occasions: no more flat rates that are the same no matter the occasion, but instead rates that better match demand on particular occasions.

Most occasions will be ordinary, so pricing will have to be cheap. But some occasions will be extraordinary and special and thus able to command a premium. These are occasions that are so special or so critical that people of every means, high and low, are virtually indifferent to price. Uber calls its premium pricing "surge pricing." But there are no "surge consumers" or "surge drivers" or "surge cars"—just "surge occasions" at which "surge pricing" applies to all consumers.

This occasion-based bifurcation of pricing is on trend with a broader economy headed high and low. Scarcity of time or money doesn't push people just to the low end; it pushes them to the high end, too. When there's only a little time or a little money to go around, spending it on something average is just as big a waste as overspending on something bad. Neither offers full value for the scarce minute or scarce dollar. To put it another way, consumers want "Superstar" offers as much as "Super-Sale" offers. Companies need a pricing proposition that unlocks both. The Uber-All business model does exactly that.

Immediacy

Another critical element of the Uber-All Economy is a shift in expectations toward immediacy. Uber and Lyft provide transportation within minutes. OpenTable books a reservation instantly. Breather and Airbnb instantly locate a room for rest, work, or play. DoorDash and Instacart get food to your door within an hour.

New expectations of immediacy are forcing established retailers to adopt on-demand models. For example, Amazon (now an established, two-decade-old retailer) has always focused on speed of delivery, from 1-Click to Prime to PrimeAir to #AmazonCart to PrimeNow. It has relentlessly chipped away at the gap between order and fulfillment. PrimeNow is Amazon's on-demand service, with two-hour delivery for free and one-hour delivery at a premium for occasions when immediacy is imperative.

Amazon is pushing the envelope even more with Amazon Dash, though. Dash was first introduced as a handheld WiFi-connected wand into which consumers speak to add an item to their AmazonFresh shopping list. Dash Button followed as a small, wireless-enabled, product-branded button that consumers press to reorder that specific product. But neither the wand nor the button push the envelope of immediacy far enough because both require consumers to go online to confirm the order. So Amazon is going a step further with Dash Replenishment Services that enable devices such as coffee makers or washing machines or printers to automatically reorder when supplies get low. This is a pioneering move in what eventually will be the norm in a world transformed by the Internet of Things.

Preemptive and even predictive ordering is not science fiction. Amazon has also filed a patent application for something it calls "anticipatory shopping software." Based on a consumer's browsing behavior, this software makes a prediction about whether a consumer is likely to buy the item being considered. If predicted to buy, Amazon will begin to ship that item before the consumer has clicked the button to buy. The future of on demand is "know demand," if you will. That is, before consumers even know they need something, machines will have placed and filled the order.

A world of Big Data and the Internet of Things will soon track consumers in real-time across all aspects of their lives. To get the most from this world, consumers will make increasing use of apps that act as personal assistants, sorting through the enormous array of options based on a profile of individual preferences. On demand will no longer be triggered by a request in the moment but by an algorithm that matches a stored profile of preferences with usage, availability, prices, and ratings.[1] These personal-assistant algorithms will adapt and improve with experience as well as push those nudges and recommendations that help people stay on track with personal goals and objectives.

From "Go To" to "Come To"

In the Uber-All Economy, the relationship between consumers and producers or retailers changes from "go to" to "come to." Heretofore, consumers have had to go to producers or retailers to initiate and complete transactions. In the Uber-All Economy, producers or retailers will come to consumers instead.

This change from "go to" to "come to" shifts costs previously borne by consumers to producers or retailers. Added costs are normally absorbed as an expense that producers or retailers push back to consumers in the form of higher prices. But in the Uber-All Economy companies may be forced to turn to different strategies for managing their margins.

Many consumers' ability to afford higher prices is uncertain in a global economy struggling with slower growth. Add to that changing expectations about immediacy as a basic requirement, not an extra benefit that is worth paying extra for. Whether consumers are able or willing to cover the costs transferred to producers or retailers will be a critical driver of the structure and shape of the Uber-All Economy.

Consumers currently must invest time and attention as part of the price they pay. They must take the time to go to the store, whether it's brick and mortar, online, or pop-up. They must take the time to browse, decide, and check out, all of which requires a great deal of attention.

In the Uber-All business model, the time and attention that were a cost paid by consumers become a cost of production for producers or retailers. Consider the half-hour it might take today for a consumer to go to the mall. In the Uber-All Economy, that is now a half-hour that producers or retailers must spend coming to a consumer. The cost of that half-hour transit time has shifted from consumers to producers or retailers. How that cost gets managed by companies is key. In all likelihood, it won't be as simple as passing it along to consumers.

Producers and retailers do things now to reduce the time and attention that consumers must spend, such as delivery, convenient locations, and express lanes. But these things are intended to reduce costs to consumers. They don't transfer those costs in whole from consumers to producers or retailers.

Consumers know the effort involved in the time and attention they spend but rarely think of it explicitly in terms of an equivalent dollar value. Because they don't pay these time and attention costs directly from their pocketbooks, to a large extent they don't see these costs. Hence, one of the key questions of the Uber-All Economy is whether consumers will be willing or able to pay with dollars for the costs of time and attention shifted to producers or retailers. Even if they are willing, they are unlikely to be able to pay enough of a premium to fully cover these shifted costs. In this case, producers and retailers won't be willing or able to sell to consumers unless they can offset these additional costs with lower costs in other parts of their business model. Finding ways to rebalance costs is what Uber-All companies are focused on the most right now. The necessity to rebalance costs due to the shift from "go to" to "come to" is driving everything else associated with the Uber-All Economy.

One of the things that will separate winners from losers in the Uber-All Economy will be ingenuity in finding ways to provide immediacy of fulfillment at an acceptable margin without raising prices. Obviously, this is an ongoing imperative in every business, but it becomes a bigger driver of success in the Uber-All Economy because of the shift from "go to" to "come to."

Technology enables Uber and other companies such as Airbnb to lower costs by leveraging underutilized assets owned by others. All on-demand mobile services keep sales costs low by using an app for ordering, payment, and feedback. But the biggest part of this rebalancing is labor costs. As an aggregation and distribution channel for people providing personal services, a company with an Uber-All business model creates scale that has been difficult to realize heretofore. In addition, by engaging people to provide personal services on demand, companies can lower the overhead costs associated with full-time employees by taking advantage of broader shifts in labor markets.

Labor Markets

Robotics and artificial intelligence (AI) are restructuring labor markets. University of Oxford technology experts Carl Frey and Michael Osborne[2] examined all job categories tracked by the U.S. Commerce Department to assess the medium-term impact of computerization. Using models that compared skills required for hundreds of individual jobs with computers' myriad capabilities, they estimated that 47 percent of all jobs in today's U.S. labor market have a 70 percent or greater likelihood of being displaced by computers over the next decade or two. This number may prove to be an underestimate because it fails to account for the likelihood that advances and practical applications in robotics and AI will begin to accelerate with more transformative impact over that same period of time.

Frey and Osborne[3] found that the jobs least likely to be displaced by technology are service jobs and "thinking jobs." This finding mirrors the future of labor markets predicted by George Mason University economist Tyler Cowen in his book *Average Is Over*.[4] Cowen argues that the only jobs safe from displacement are jobs for people running technology or jobs for people selling personal services to the people running technology.

There is a great deal of uncertainty about whether displacement means permanent job losses. By and large, economic historians read the record of technological disruption as one of short-term losses more than offset by long-term gains. But this time the outcome may be different. The complex of jobs associated with technology will not be as robust as they were previously. Horses and buggies couldn't take care of horses and buggies. That was a job for people. Similarly, cars can't take care of cars; airplanes can't take care of airplanes; personal computers can't take care of personal computers; and so forth. But robots will soon enough be able to take care of robots. AI is already self-referential and self-learning. Humans will be needed less and less. In previous eras, technology was engineered to make human toil unnecessary, but now technology is being engineered to make humans unnecessary.

As far as the Uber-All Economy is concerned, though, it matters only that technology is changing the types of jobs that remain for people to do. There may be more or fewer jobs, but the jobs available will be either jobs running technology or jobs selling personal services. The Uber-All business model is built on precisely this two-fold mix of job skills, making it a perfect analogue for the future of work and thus a natural complement to macrolevel changes in labor markets.

The Uber-All Ecosystem

As on-demand mobile services become the dominant business model, a number of other things will spin out of this transformation. A few are worth a short headline here and greater consideration elsewhere.

Investors and entrepreneurs will focus more attention on existing assets and infrastructure. Owners of existing assets will benefit from new income streams, but less in the form of traditional rents and more in the form of shared profits from greater utilization.

This change in focus will spill over into regulatory policy. The search for new uses or greater utilization of existing assets and infrastructure will strengthen economic and political pressure against regulations that limit or proscribe uses and utilization.

Consumer markets will experience a decline in variety seeking and impulse buying as personal-assistant algorithms tied to preference profiles become commonplace. Although novelty and experimentation may be programmed as a preference, producers will resist it. They will look to lock in dedicated choices in their deals with device manufacturers and software programmers. Plus, consumers will be reluctant to experiment with new things sight unseen.

Algorithms tied to preference profiles will narrow consideration sets considerably, perhaps even rendering that marketing metric irrelevant. As a result, awareness and trial will shift from marketing channels to lifestyle events in which sampling and virtual experimentation are woven into the entertainment.

Trust will be distributed and secured from the bottom up by community consensus, not from the top down by authority or heritage. Reputation will be tracked by real-time ratings that can be accessed in the moment by personal-assistant algorithms.

With the Uber-All Economy comes a new value proposition that has social ramifications beyond the consumer marketplace per se. The nature and meaning of work will be most affected, which may be the most hopeful aspect of this economic transformation. If everyone is embedded in a social context fundamentally grounded in service relationships rather than in the manufacturing and marketing of goods, then networks of connection and contact will be a more pervasive part of life, rekindling community and nurturing relationships, long known to be the most profound sources of happiness and satisfaction with life.

11

Tomorrow 3.0

The Sharing Economy

Michael C. Munger

RIGHT NOW, WE own stuff. I do, you do, the people across the street who can't get their car in the garage do . . . we own a ton of stuff. The self-storage industry in the United States has nearly fifty thousand facilities, with more than 15 billion cubic feet of space[1] cluttered with . . . stuff.

But people don't fundamentally want *stuff*. What they want is the *stream of services* that stuff provides over time. So if people own stuff—clothes, tools, cars, houses—rather than rent that stuff, it is because owning secures services more reliably and at lower transaction costs than renting. But this "preference" for owning is not real. It might change quickly if entrepreneurs were able to figure out a way to sell reductions in transaction costs.

And that's the thesis of this essay. The future will look very different from the past and the present because in the future entrepreneurs *will have* figured out how to sell reductions in transaction costs. Almost everything we own will soon be a potential rental item, or we won't own it at all because we'll rent it from someone else. And (almost) everything will be better. Except for the things that will be worse.

Revolution Is Disruptive

There have been two enormous "revolutions" in human history. The first was the Neolithic Revolution, or the wide-scale switch from a nomadic hunter-gatherer lifestyle to fixed agriculture. The second was the Industrial Revolution, or the wide-scale concentration of production in processes that took advantage of division of labor and capital-intensive work. The most salient feature of both revolutions was unprecedented expansion: after the Neolithic

Revolution, cities developed, and populations increased in ways that transformed the landscape.

After the Industrial Revolution, production processes developed in ways that within just a few generations afforded a set of consumer items for the poor that had been unattainable even for the wealthy just a century earlier. So where the Neolithic Revolution resulted in an explosion of population, the Industrial Revolution resulted in an explosion of capital accumulation and cheap consumer products.

Jared Diamond[2] called the move to fixed agriculture a "mistake," perhaps tongue in cheek. Still, it is true that liberty, nutrition, and hygiene suffered. But for something to be a mistake there has to have been an alternative. For both revolutions, things could not have been otherwise. Suppose we grant that people were individually worse off for a few generations at least. The consequences of realizing economies of scale in military action and the benefits of access to the products of increased specialization overwhelmed the ability of any but the most isolated tribes to choose any other form of society.[3]

Adam Smith summarized the larger economic reasons that division of labor is important, and Émile Durkheim and others later echoed it. The title of chapter 3 of book 1 of *The Wealth of Nations* puts it this way: "That the Division of Labor Is Limited by the Extent of the Market."[4] Returns to scale are not linear in terms of the "size" of society. Rather, the nature and quality of the products and services available have dramatic and increasing returns to scale.

This conclusion is so obvious that it escapes our attention most of the time. In a tribe of one hundred, there may be someone who is skilled at beating bones on a rock. In a clan of one thousand, there may be someone who can play a flute and others who can manipulate a string tightened on a bent piece of wood. In a city of one hundred thousand, there are chamber orchestras. And in a city of one million there is a symphony, with highly specialized instruments and people who make a living playing or repairing those instruments. The tribe couldn't support a symphony, and the expectations of the city's citizens are too advanced to be satisfied with the guy beating bones on a rock. Of course, the same thing goes for coercion. If you are a tribe of hunter-gatherers, your "army" of forty adult males will be overwhelmed by the ten thousand trained warriors from the city on the other side of the mountains. There is no hope of resistance, so you settle down to farm. The choices were either to accept the consequences—economic, political, and social—or cease to exist.

The third revolution will be like that, too. And it has already started.

Tomorrow 3.0

The two previous revolutions made each of us more dependent on all of us, though perhaps in a good way. I could specialize in some narrow activity because I could rely on other people to specialize in producing all the other things I needed, from food to the nice woolen coat Adam Smith made famous as an example. Smith's point, which is even more true today, is that each of us can afford more *and* better stuff because of specialization.

But we still rely, even in the best circumstances, on ownership. We end up with far more stuff than any of us actually need or could use. We store the stuff in closets, garages, cupboards, and "U-Store" facilities. The result is that we have to pay the *average* cost of everything—pretty much everything.

Why not just pay the *marginal* cost rather than the *average* cost? After all, if I own an apartment, I'm already paying for utilities and making mortgage payments. But what if I'm not always there or if I have an extra room I almost never use except for storing junk? I would be willing—maybe even happy—to offer someone else my place to stay for whatever I can get to pay toward my fixed costs and the cost of having to clean it afterward. If I can actually get more than my fixed costs, I would be pleased to offer the apartment for rent.

I'm willing to offer rides at the cost of gas, my time, and wear and tear on the vehicle. It's also true that density helps both buyer and seller because waiting times are reduced as more people use a service. Overall, a "shared" apartment owned and often occupied by someone else can provide lodging services far more cheaply and still benefit both parties.

The reason we don't see more sharing is "transaction costs."[5] If I go to bars or perhaps to street corners in Raleigh, North Carolina, and ask random strangers if they want to spend the night at my place, the experiment won't go very well. (Don't ask me how I know that; just take my word for it!) And it won't go much better if I walk around in some other city and ask folks if I can spend the night with them. (Again, don't ask how I know that.) But it's perfectly true that there are some people who have extra room and others who need a place to stay in a strange city. What's missing is (1) information about identity and location; (2) a way of making payment that both parties can trust; and (3) a way of outsourcing trust on performance of the terms of the contract.

The usual answer to this problem is "hotels," of course. But hotels are expensive because they have to cover their average costs: all of their expenses are involved in the business of selling rooms by the night. That's not true of apartments or homes where people live because those other expenses are being paid already. The price required to make the seller willing to rent a room or an apartment during the summer when they are away is much lower.

That arrangement is better for the buyer also, of course, as long as the three components listed earlier can be satisfied reliably. It isn't easy for seller and buyer to find each other, make a payment transfer, and outsource trust at a reasonable cost. Of course, because of Airbnb and other home-"sharing" software platforms, that's no longer true. And the existing stock of "stuff" can be used far more efficiently. As transaction costs fall—which means as entrepreneurs find new ways to "sell" reductions in transaction costs—much of what we now own will change its status. All of us will rent more and own less. Some of us may specialize in being "sellers" in these new rental markets for things we do own. But, overall, each of us will have actual possession of far, far less stuff at any given time.

From Owning to Renting, from Companies to People

We are used to thinking of getting stuff from companies or firms that own products or provide services. This model is changing in two ways that are connected but distinct. The first change is the move from owning to renting. The second change is the ability to transact peer to peer instead of business to consumer. The interaction between these two changes will have far-reaching implications.

From Companies to People

The biggest change in the software-platform-driven revolution in transaction costs is that people will skip companies except as middlemen. We are already used to this jump with Airbnb and Uber, both of which provide access to privately owned services (rooms and rides, respectively) for private citizens. All the software does is provide information, take care of security (through ratings and reputation), and process the transaction (removing most of the risk of robbery or reneging).

But there are hundreds of other examples for stuff you may not have thought of renting. One company, Spinlister, brings together people who have but currently aren't using bikes, surf equipment, and ski equipment and people who need those things. All three of these goods are relatively durable, sometimes not used for long periods, and expensive. For instance, Rent Luggage is Uber for luggage and expensive hiking gear. Private individuals have stuff. Other private individuals need the stuff for a short period. With high transaction costs, the choices previously were either to buy the stuff (expensive in terms of cash and storage) or to do without it. If an entrepreneur can sell the reduction in transaction cost through a software platform, private individuals will make much more intensive use of the stuff they already have.

In a short time, the result will be that many of us will have much less stuff. I won't need to own a laptop, a bike, a car, luggage . . . or maybe even clothes. A company called RentTheRunway rents "unlimited clothing and accessories" for $99 per month. The offer is not really unlimited, of course. Customers (it's supposed to be for women, but to each her or his own) can have only one of each item per category at a time. But when the customer is finished with the dress or shoes or purse, he or she sends it back. RentTheRunway takes care of the shipping and the dry cleaning.

The Dark Side

The good news is that we all will own and store much less stuff. The bad news is that . . . well, that's the bad news, too. An economy in which entrepreneurs have always been focused on making new products or on making more old products more inexpensively will be shaken to its foundations.

Instead of 90 million power drills sitting in closets and garages, we'll need only 10 million because we'll be able to rent rather than own a drill. The drills will be more expensive and sturdy, commercial rentals rather than cheap consumer models. But the decline in production-line requirements will be enormous. We'll need far fewer cars (and much less real estate devoted to parking), fewer bikes, fewer hotel complexes—less of just about everything.

But some people, probably many people, will lose their jobs. And they won't get new jobs, at least jobs in the sense that we understand them. They may work "gigs" or temporary periods as parts of teams, the way the construction industry or Broadway plays operate now.

Will this change be good or bad? As in the previous two revolutions, that hardly matters because the economic logic is inescapable: it's just going to happen. Nevertheless, I think it's fair to say that for most people the effect will be positive because although nominal wages may fall, the quality-adjusted price level will fall by more, implying an actual increase in real wages.

Not least, the effects on the environment, considered broadly, will be largely positive. Cities won't need parking spaces or underground garage spaces. Houses won't need garages or nearly as many closets. Energy use in manufacturing and the amount of waste produced from packaging and discarding broken or unused products will plummet.

If Andy Warhol were alive today, he might describe the new world this way: in the future, people will own stuff for fifteen minutes.

12

Bitcoin and the Future
of Digital Payments

William J. Luther

FOLLOWING THE PUBLICATION of a white paper by Satoshi Nakamoto in 2008, bitcoin was quietly introduced to the world in 2009 as not much more than an obscure piece of code. For more than a year after its introduction, each bitcoin in circulation traded for pennies as a community of coders made minor modifications and refinements to the open-source client at the system's core. Its value climbed to roughly $1.00 by February 2011 and then to nearly $30 four months later before settling down to an average of just $8.16 from July 2011 to February 2012. After that, demand began to increase. First gradually. Then suddenly.

In mid-2015, one bitcoin exchanges for roughly $290. It is accepted by a wide variety of businesses around the world, from major online retailers to food trucks. An entire cottage industry has emerged to help individuals buy, sell, store, transfer, and track the price of bitcoin. It is routinely the subject of major media coverage. And everyone with even a passing interest in bitcoin seems to have one question in mind: Will it survive?

Opinions regarding the future of bitcoin are mixed. Jennifer Shasky Calvery, the director of the Financial Crimes Enforcement Network, suggests bitcoin could become "a significant player in the financial system."[1] Others express optimism regarding the underlying blockchain technology but reserve judgment on bitcoin in particular. Nassim Taleb, for example, believes "[b]itcoin is the beginning of something great: a currency without a government, something necessary and imperative." However, he remains unsure "whether [bitcoin] is the best potential setup" and recognizes that it takes "a long time to establish confidence" in a new payment system.[2] Still others see little hope for bitcoin. Although Paul Krugman acknowledges that bitcoin solves "an interesting information problem," he doubts "whether solving that problem has any economic value."[3]

In this essay, I consider the factors affecting the likelihood that bitcoin will continue to facilitate exchange in the future. First, I discuss the obstacles to bitcoin from incumbent monies and alt-coins. Then I offer my view on the future of bitcoin and digital payments.

Bitcoin and the Incumbent-Monies Problem

The biggest obstacle to the widespread adoption of bitcoin is the incumbent-monies problem. Virtually everyone in the world is already using money. Therefore, the decision to use bitcoin is, at least on the margin, the decision to stop using an incumbent money. The problem: switching costs and network effects favor the status quo.[4]

Switching costs refer to any cost required to transition from the incumbent money to bitcoin. They include the need to retool vending and automatic teller machines; to update menus and transaction records; and even to learn to think and calculate in terms of a new unit of account. If bitcoin is to have any hope of replacing an incumbent money, it must be sufficiently better to warrant the cost of switching.[5]

Network effects result when the value of a good or service depends on the total number of those using it. Monies are characterized by network effects because a medium of exchange is useful only to the extent that one's trading partners are willing to accept it. Moreover, when one is choosing between multiple monies (or would-be monies), historical acceptance might act as a particularly salient focal point for coordinating on the incumbent money.[6] Hence, even if bitcoin warrants the costs of switching, it must also be sufficiently better than an incumbent money (net of switching costs) to warrant the costs of coordination.[7]

The incumbent-monies problem is exacerbated by the fact that virtually all incumbent monies employed at present are government sponsored. These monies typically benefit from some form of legal-tender status and public receivability (i.e., the government accepts taxes in and makes payments with the incumbent money). By providing a lower bound on the network size of the incumbent money, legal-tender status and public receivability make it more difficult to overcome the network-effects problem.[8]

Government-sponsored incumbent monies also permit the issuer to conduct monetary policy, generate seigniorage revenue, and, at least with electronic balances, provide some scope for oversight and confiscation. To the extent that bitcoin conflicts with governmental objectives (e.g., conducting monetary policy, raising revenue, preventing private agents from engaging in illegal transactions, protecting private agents from fraud, etc.), it might be subject to regulatory efforts aimed at precluding or dissuading users from adopting it.[9] Indeed, some governments have already taken steps to ban or regulate bitcoin.[10] And as Reuben Grinberg explains, even the absence of explicit regulation "may significantly hamper demand" because ambiguity leaves bitcoin "in a legal grey area."[11] Hence, the regulatory environment— be it explicit or implicit—might significantly raise the costs of switching to bitcoin for some users.

Competition from Alt-Coins

In addition to the challenge posed by incumbent monies, bitcoin also faces competition from other cryptocurrencies, otherwise known as alt-coins. Like bitcoin, alt-coins face the incumbent-monies problem. They also have to overcome bitcoin's first-mover advantage. However, alt-coins might make use of a second-mover advantage to outcompete bitcoin in the long run.

Alt-coins exploded onto the scene shortly after bitcoin's early (if limited) success.[12] There are more than five hundred cryptocurrencies trading today, with a combined market capitalization of roughly $4.89 billion as of July 15, 2015.[13] Bitcoin dominates the market by far: with a market capitalization of $4.17 billion, it holds 85.6 percent of the market. Notable alt-coins include ripple ($274 million; 5.6 percent), litecoin ($183 million; 3.7 percent), dash ($21 million; 0.42 percent), and dogecoin ($19 million; 0.39 percent). Lawrence White reports that the market caps of ripple and litecoin were 8.5 percent and 1.8 percent as large as bitcoin on March 9, 2015.[14] As of July 15, 2015, they are 6.6 percent and 4.4 percent, respectively.

The success of bitcoin relative to other cryptocurrencies suggests it enjoys a substantial first-mover advantage. If one is interested in switching to a cryptocurrency, bitcoin is the obvious choice. It is the most familiar, so it enjoys relatively lower switching costs, and it has the biggest network. In other words, the same forces that discourage users from switching from incumbent monies to bitcoin encourage those users that have already switched to stick with bitcoin and those users who are going to switch to choose bitcoin over one of its alt-coin rivals. This state of affairs bodes well for bitcoin.

However, alt-coins might enjoy a second-mover advantage. Specifically, developers can identify common complaints about bitcoin and offer alt-coins that are modified to address the issues. For example, litecoin employs the same proof-of-work distribution as bitcoin, but it offers a maximum circulation of 84 million coins, whereas bitcoin is limited to 21 million. Similarly, a relatively new alt-coin aptly named NuBits ($0.55 million market capitalization; 0.01 percent of the market) overcomes purchasing-power volatility issues experienced by bitcoin by pegging its value to the dollar.[15] Whether and to what extent the second-mover advantage enjoyed by some alt-coins will be sufficient to overcome the incumbent-money problem and bitcoin's first-mover advantage remain to be seen.

The Future of Digital Payments

Predicting the future in the face of technological change is almost certainly a fool's errand. A decade and a half ago eBay was king, and Amazon sold books. The popular romantic comedy *You've Got Mail*[16] saw the owner of a small local bookstore match with the heir of a megabookstore chain likely to put her out of business. Barnes & Noble had sued Amazon in 1997 for claiming to be "the world's largest bookstore," and yet few questioned the plot. Looking back, it seems obvious that Amazon would push out not only the small local bookstore but also the megabookstore chains and many other brick-and-mortar shops that sell a wide range of products. But it was not so obvious at the time. The Internet was neat. It made it easier to chat with loved ones and find new friends. However, it was difficult to imagine in the late 1990s all the ways in which it would touch our day-to-day lives in the future—let alone which companies would come to dominate the landscape. Much the same might be said about the future of digital payments today. Nevertheless, and perhaps against my better judgment, I offer some modest predictions based at least in part on the forces discussed earlier.

The share of electronic transactions will continue to increase. The share of the currency component of M1 to the M1 money stock peaked in October 2007 at 56 percent. Today, it sits around 42 percent because people are somewhat less inclined to use currency to make transactions. Why? In part because of the rise in online shopping and in part because it has never been more convenient to make digital payments in face-to-face exchanges. With the widespread adoption of smartphones and the relatively recent rollout of small, low-fee card-reader devices by Square, PayPal, and others, even the smallest business can accept electronic payments. And, more recently, smartphone apps such as Venmo and Cash (by Square) enable users to make digital payments on the fly with virtually anyone else willing to download the app. As existing vending machines, parking meters, card readers, and the like are replaced with newer, tap-to-pay-enabled devices, it will become even easier to make digital payments. In the future, the rare occasion when one asks a stranger or shopkeeper if she has change for a dollar (or, given inflation, perhaps a five or a ten) will provide an amusing reminder of a time when cash was king and transacting was much less convenient.

The blockchain technology will be widely adopted to process digital payments. The technological advance of bitcoin is its ability to process transactions over a distributed network without a central node functioning as a bank or clearinghouse.[17] At the moment, processing transactions using the blockchain seems to be less costly than the traditional approach. Moreover, the business of processing transactions tends to be highly concentrated. As such, the volume of transactions handled by each payment processor means that the benefit of switching might be quite large, and the small number of participants means that the cost of coordinating to overcome network effects is probably small. Hence, to the extent that the blockchain technology lowers transaction costs, it will likely be adopted to process digital payments.

Some businesses have already taken steps toward adopting the blockchain technology. NASDAQ announced it will launch a blockchain-style digital-ledger technology to manage equities with its NASDAQ Private Market platform.[18] The consulting firm Deloitte has established the Deloitte Crypto-currency Community to advise its customers on the benefits of the blockchain for exchanging funds and managing staff payments, among other things.[19] Even the U.S. Federal Reserve System[20] has looked into the blockchain—or what it calls a "digital value transfer vehicle"—to process interbank payments. More firms will likely adopt the technology as it becomes more familiar.

Bitcoin and other cryptocurrencies, to the extent that they survive at all, will likely function exclusively as niche monies. Most users seem relatively content with the existing payment system. They perceive the benefits of switching to be small. And, with so many potential trading partners, the costs of coordination are quite large. So although the blockchain technology will likely be adopted to process transactions on the back end, the average consumer will not switch from incumbent money to cryptocurrency.

Some users might experience large gains from switching to a cryptocurrency if it enables them to complete transactions they would otherwise be unable to complete. For example, the extent to which bitcoin permits pseudonymous transactions seems to make it especially useful in illicit transactions. It was the only currency accepted on the Silk Road, an online marketplace where users could buy illegal goods and services from 2011 to 2013.[21] Most online illicit markets in operation today also rely on cryptocurrencies.

Others have suggested that cryptocurrencies might provide a convenient mechanism for monetizing contributions that are currently zero priced. Because cryptocurrencies are usually divisible to many decimal places—eight in the case of bitcoin—users might offer very small tips when viewing online content. Facebook permits apps enabling users to offer others tips in cryptocurrency.[22] As in the case of illegal transactions, however, these benefits are limited to a subset of one's transactions. Hence, bitcoin or some other alt-coin might find some limited success functioning as a niche money even if it is not adopted more widely.

Bitcoin or some other cryptocurrency might function as more than a niche money in countries with especially weak currencies, even though these countries would seem to pose the greatest regulatory risk to bitcoin. The most likely place for a cryptocurrency to accomplish widespread acceptance would seem to be where the incumbent money is managed poorly because in these cases the benefits might be sufficiently high to warrant the costs of switching and coordination. Individuals have historically been reluctant to switch currencies to such an extent—even in the absence of legal restrictions—except in cases of hyperinflation or government support.[23] And, when they have switched, they tend to prefer the currency of their largest trading partners and/or a widely accepted, fairly stable currency such as the dollar or the euro. In the future, however, cryptocurrencies might thrive in such an environment because, unlike the paper-money alternatives, they allow users to make digital payments. In Kenya, where many people are unbanked but have cell phones, Vodafone's m-pesa system has taken off.[24] If the incumbent money were especially unstable, such users might opt to use their phones to transfer cryptocurrencies instead.

One countervailing force in such environments is the prospect for outright bans or excessive regulation. Governments that mismanage currencies tend to institute other draconian measures when things go awry. Nonetheless, the few cases of unofficial currency substitution in the face of troubled currencies provide some reason to believe those wishing to use cryptocurrencies might successfully circumvent the law. Similarly, the few cases of official currency substitution and currency boards suggest that some governments are willing to take drastic actions—and sacrifice seigniorage—when few options remain. As such, there is some hope for the widespread adoption of cryptocurrencies in countries with especially weak currencies.

Conclusion

Bitcoin represents a technological advance in the processing of payments. It is always difficult to predict the future, but technological advancements tend to be put to good use—at least until something better comes along. In my opinion, the long-run odds do not seem to favor bitcoin—or any other existing cryptocurrency, for that matter. One can, however, be reasonably certain regarding the growth of electronic transactions. And if the blockchain technology significantly reduces the costs of processing transactions, it will be adopted. As for bitcoin and the alt-coins it has inspired, they are unlikely to function as more than a niche money except in the unlikely event of hyperinflation or government support or both.

13

The Connected Home and an Electricity-Market Platform for the Twenty-First Century

L. Lynne Kiesling

IT'S THE START of a new week. Monday morning, the alarm that wakes you up is a gentle, increasingly glowing full-spectrum LED light timed to wake you up refreshed and on schedule and connected to sensors embedded in your pillow that determine where you are in your sleep cycle. As you stand up, the motion sensor in your bedroom alerts the vacuum-packed coffee bean storage in the kitchen to grind the beans and brew your first cup of coffee just the way you like it. You press the shower button, and the on-demand electric water heater gives you a shower at the precise temperature you prefer, a setting that you can change seasonally or leave alone, as you prefer. The coffee maker, water heater, and shower may also have used Bayesian learning to record the patterns of your morning routine without the need for any explicit programming on your part. The devices learn your patterns and just work, yielding a quality of life that was not possible before.

You may also choose to time the water heating (and perhaps your shower, if you have a flexible schedule) based on the price you pay for electricity; you have programmed in your trigger prices in your home-management system, and if the price forecast for your usual shower time is higher than the trigger price, the water heater can preheat water for your shower, saving you money with no loss of comfort or convenience. The same functionality exists in your home's heating and cooling system as well as in the major energy-consuming and energy-producing appliances and devices in your home.

You have contracted with a home-services retailer to provide you with a bundled network service for communication, entertainment, home security, and energy, and you have choice among several retailers. The services for which you contract and the way that you pay for those services will be diverse, and you can customize your services as much or as little as you prefer.

The next fifty years will involve increasing human interaction with digital technology as the Internet of Things grows and more devices have more embedded intelligence and automation capabilities. The alarm clock starting the coffee maker is a colorful illustration of the extent and depth to which the Internet of Things will change how individuals interact with the physical environment, and with each other. Many of these changes will occur in the home, intersecting with the consumption and increasingly with the production of electricity.

Some of these capabilities already exist and are not fifty years in the future. In-home technologies such as the Nest thermostat use Bayesian learning to figure out habitation patterns and adjust home temperatures accordingly. Connecting the Nest thermostat with the Nest smoke/carbon monoxide detector and remote-control LED lightbulbs enables improved safety and home security, and temperature and lighting can be automated and adjusted using a mobile-device app. Whirlpool has created a line of Whirlpool Smart laundry appliances and an accompanying mobile-device app to control the timing of laundry cycles and their energy use. Not all of these innovations have demonstrated value to consumers yet, but they may.

Innovation aligning economic and environmental incentives also comes from the evolution of the connected home. Imagine, for example, customizing the built environment with digital sensors that enable preset and automated lighting, air conditioning, or refrigerator changes automatically as electricity prices change or when renewable power becomes available. Technologies already exist to make some of these capabilities possible, and innovation is bringing about more of them.

In all aspects of daily life, digital technologies have reduced transaction costs, enabled deeper and richer decentralized exchange (think of automatic teller machines, online commerce, Uber, and Airbnb as examples), and fostered a greater ability to automate routine interactions (e.g., Amazon's Subscribe and Save feature). In the built environment, digital technologies and their powerful decentralizing and transaction-cost-reducing forces align economic and environmental values, enabling individuals to save money and increase environmental quality by using digital technologies to optimize their energy consumption and production.

These economic and environmental benefits arise in part out of the ability to automate actions and transactions. The British philosopher Alfred North Whitehead famously observed that "[c]ivilization advances by extending the number of important operations which we can perform without thinking of them,"[1] and F. A. Hayek observed similarly, "The more civilized we become, the more relatively ignorant must each individual be of the facts on which the working of his civilization depends."[2]

Looking into the next fifty years of electricity and technology involves several deep unknowns. In 2015, the long-awaited and much-vaunted development of more economical energy-storage technologies is accelerating. Combined with innovation in distributed generation, storage innovation is likely to be a substantial disruptor that will change electricity consumption and production over the next five decades. Both solar photovoltaic technologies and electric vehicle technologies have in the past five years improved in energy efficiency and decreased production costs, although based on cost alone they cannot yet match mature fossil-fuel technologies.

Although Vaclav Smil[3] is correct that there is no Moore's Law for energy technologies as exists for communication technologies, further research and innovation in distributed energy and storage will change the scale at which electricity can be generated economically. The last time this happened was in the late 1980s, when the combined-cycle gas turbine undercut the monolithic economies of scale in generation and prompted regulatory change to allow competitive wholesale markets and spur the unbundling of generation from the vertically integrated, regulated utility in several states.

These innovations change not just the economies of scale in generation but also the nature of the transactions themselves. Distributed resources and storage make the residential consumer both consumer and producer, which means that a more decentralized retail market is possible rather than the traditional monolithic linear supply chain from the vertically integrated firm to end-use consumers. The potential for a highly decentralized retail market for electricity is amplified further by digital smart-grid technologies, which make interconnection easier, more automated, and less likely to create imbalances and outages in the distribution grid. Digital smart-grid technologies also enable the interconnection of increasingly heterogeneous devices across a network of homes and other buildings. These buildings and devices are owned and operated by increasingly heterogeneous types and sizes of agents. A homeowner can own an electric vehicle or a residential rooftop solar, enabling both consumption and generation of electricity. Microgrids can connect a neighborhood of individuals and technologies capable of consuming or generating or both, at both large and small scales.

These technological innovations also change the potential for another wave of competitive markets and unbundling, this time in competitive retail markets and the unbundling of retail service from the distribution-wires network, which at least in the near term is likely to retain its economies of scale. The markets, business models, and regulatory institutions that will emerge are also unknown; they will depend on the nature and pace of innovation, the political economy of unwinding a regulated industry heavily invested in the status quo, and the extent to which the culture of consumers, producers, and regulators embraces an attitude of permissionless innovation.[4]

One final unknown is the extent to which these innovations will induce residential electricity consumers to use distributed resources and storage for self-sufficiency and thus go "off-grid" rather than stay connected to the distribution grid. Consumers leaving the grid reduces revenue to the regulated wires owner. Whether regulators and utilities can bring about changes to make the distribution grid connection valuable in an environment with distributed resources will be a significant challenge in the next two decades. Transitioning into a role as the distribution grid operator and market platform provider (and not a market participant) would enable the wires company to earn revenue by facilitating mutually beneficial transactions and by providing transaction fulfillment through coordination of multidirectional energy flows.

In electricity, as in other industries, digital communication technology makes it possible and easy to have two-way communication and to use that communication capability to automate individual actions. As we have seen throughout society, the proliferation of communication technology makes it easier and cheaper to engage in transactions. The implications for the electric power network are a rich transactional environment, a market platform, and a network connecting producers and consumers who contract and negotiate their mutual exchange of value (product, service) for value (payment). A smart grid is a transactive grid.

Digital technologies can make the electric power network transactive over the next fifty years. These technologies, though, are necessary but not sufficient—an economically (and environmentally) sustainable electric power network in 2065 will also require institutional change. Except for municipal water, electricity remains the most heavily economically regulated of the infrastructure industries, and this economic regulation has to this point focused on universal electrification and low, stable prices for a standard commodity service. Regulation creates entry barriers in retail electricity markets in most states in the United States, and in the states that do have retail markets for residential customers, some persistent features of regulation have entrenched entry barriers and incumbent vertical market power.[5] The traditional focus of regulation on investment in generation and wires assets means that both regulators and regulated utilities have a significant status quo bias.

Retail entry barriers and status quo bias mean barriers to innovation. Market entry remains the most potent process for creativity and new value creation in the form of technological change and product differentiation. Regulatory institutions are not adaptive and generally do not deal well with change, in particular the effects of technological change. They arose in and are conditioned to a specific social-technological context that has been changing over the past two decades due to the decentralizing forces of digital technology. The policy challenges and objectives present in the twentieth century have receded and been reprioritized along with new policy challenges: providing incentives to innovate and adopt new technologies, providing the type of customer choice and decentralized decision-making capabilities that consumers experience in nearly all other aspects of their lives, managing the environmental consequences of electricity consumption, and maintaining reliable service in the face of consistent, pervasive change.

If retail regulatory institutions do not allow firms the freedom to enter or consumers the freedom to choose how much price risk to bear and what price signals to receive, then they fail to deliver on the dynamic value-creating potential of the smart grid as a transactive market platform that enables the connected homes of the future to be assets for exchange.

14

If Government Were Angels, Only Humans Would Be Necessary

A Look at the Economic Prospects of 2065

Brian F. Domitrovic

TO ASK THE historian what the economy will be like fifty years from now is to invite comparisons to fifty years ago. As I write in the summer of 2015, weeks before the half-century anniversary of the Watts riots in Los Angeles, fifty years ago was 1965—the very acme of American economic history. A friend of mine, Louis Woodhill, is an entrepreneur and a blogger. Holman Jenkins of the *Wall Street Journal* once wrote that the reaction to one of Woodhill's blogs questioning the General Motors bailout was "one of those kerfuffles that render the Web a net plus."[1] Woodhill has told me that he realized that 1965 was the acme of American prosperity when he acquired a superlative Pontiac Bonneville convertible from that year. "Note the exuberant styling," Woodhill wrote to me recently, verbally pointing to a picture of the car, a broad, black beauty. "No other country ever produced anything like the American cars of 1965, and especially not for ordinary people. In 1965, a man with a decent blue-collar job could support a family at a middle-class level. He also had reason to be optimistic about the future."

The American with a job had reason to be optimistic about the future in 1965 because of the trend perceptible at that point. The thing about trends, however, is that you can never quite tell which one you are riding. Are you on an exponential curve or a wave? In small sections, but only in small sections, the two paths are identical. The slope of an exponential curve is exactly that of a wave as the wave climbs out of its trough, reaching toward its peak, but a peak (as well as the inflection toward the peak) is something that an exponential curve does not have. As it turned out, the year 1965—before the Watts riots began in August—was the last moment that the wavelike nature of the trend of American prosperity was consistent with an exponential curve. After that, the trend of economic growth and its dissemination slowed and then reversed course, with variation since then, such that 2015 does not extrapolate from 1965 on the basis of what one saw burgeoning all around the nation in 1965 and in the years immediately preceding it.

The raw, blunderbuss numbers give a rosy picture of 1965. Gross domestic product (GDP) was growing by 6 percent, expanding on the 5 percent growth of the previous three years. The unemployment rate (a lagging economic indicator) was a little less than 5 percent and set to dip to less than 4 percent the next year. The number of employed Americans (also a lagging indicator) was halfway through an increase of 13 million from 1961 to 1969. The inflation rate was 1.6 percent. The Dow industrials crossed 1,000 for the first time in January 1966, a level not exceeded in real terms until the 1990s. And federal government spending went down, not only in real but in nominal terms, from 1964 to 1965—the last time that would happen for forty-five years.

The year 1965 was the locus classicus of "postwar prosperity"—the most cherished and beloved era of all U.S. economic history, those "glorious years" (as the French call them) still talked about today nostalgically by many, even those born after 1965. Nonetheless, there were things about the prosperity of 1965 that were fully perceptible at the time and that did not suggest an exponential curve, but rather a wave. Prior to 1961, the economy had been nothing special. From 1949 to 1960, there were four recessions, one of them, in 1957–58, containing a six-month drop in economic output of 7 percent per annum. Over the years of Dwight D. Eisenhower's presidency (1953–61), the nation added all of 4 million jobs even as the working-age population surged by 7 million. The biggest nonfiction paperback best seller to date, Michael Harrington's *The Other America*,[2] argued that the serial recessions of the 1950s and early 1960s had created a structural class of poor that possibly numbered 50 million.

Our nostalgia for postwar prosperity has often led to the assumption that the 1950s were economically stupendous. Progressive intellectuals and politicians perpetuate this assumption, speaking—as President Barack Obama's top economist Jason Furman[3] does—of the "golden age from 1948 to 1973," probably because that characterization enables the argument that the 91 percent marginal income-tax rate, which held till 1963, was consistent with a legendary general prosperity. This argument is misleading. The 1950s and the early 1960s were mediocre at best with respect to the standards of U.S. economic performance. The economic growth that came after 1961 and held even until 1969 was a stellar run touched off with a tax cut, a recommitment to the gold dollar, and shrunken government spending—the policy choices of the three years from 1962 to 1964—that made possible the concept of postwar prosperity in the first place.[4]

So the year 1965 pointed to nothing but progress along a wave, part of one period in a cycle: the Roaring Twenties, the Great Depression of the 1930s, the postwar boom of the 1940s, the serial recessions of the 1950s, the boom of the 1960s. Of course, the 1970s were going to be the stagflation decade. Odds would have it that there would be an economic resurgence in the 1980s. If that resurgence stayed through the 1990s, there would come fifteen years of "secular stagnation" after 2000. The frequency of the wave of economic performance stretched out a little after 1980.

And yet the trajectory of economic performance in 1965 *was* that of an exponential curve—because a wave's first ascent is consistent with an exponential curve. If the performance of the years immediately before 1965 had maintained itself after 1965, sustained economic growth (not a wave) would have been the legacy. Something must have enforced the wavelike quality of unsustained growth, something structural or the workings of an outside agency. Otherwise, the exponential function would have taken over.

That year also happened to be the year that Mancur Olson, perhaps the greatest political scientist of the century, published *The Logic of Collective Action*. This pillar of public-choice economics came to represent the general thesis of that field—namely, that government strives to take what it can from the real sector of the economy and develops talents and skills in that direction. In 1965, the U.S. economy was presenting the government with the prospect of crisis, specifically an existential crisis. If the economy continued to grow at the stunning rate of 6 percent, as federal spending went down in real terms, the government would begin to lose its grip on existence. A decade or two of 60 to 70 percent private-sector growth in the face of shrinking government would make the government irrelevant, powerless. The nation would be its own, unformed by the government.

What perhaps happened after 1965 is that government, like any canny evolutionary entity, unconsciously realized that circumstances were endangering it, which compelled it to take steps to solidify its existence. These steps took both positive and negative forms, including policies that would slow the rate of private-sector growth and policies (often coextensive) that would enhance the size and impress of government. Clear examples are the tax increases of 1968 and thereafter, the buildup of welfare and regulation, and the move toward a purely fiat money system. Other examples may well include the government's encouragement of the "great crime wave" from 1965 to around 1980 (by means of overcriminalization along with excessive leniency on the part of progressive judges), whose major effect since 1980 has been the rise of the American police state.

In 2015, private-sector economic growth is perhaps 2 percent; total government displacement of the economy is a third greater than it was in 1965; major industries such as banking and auto manufacture are wards of the state; and the stagnation experience is so persistent that the dropouts from the labor force in the past decade number almost 10 million. Government, however, has had little problem collecting taxes, funding its debts, taking on workers, and expanding its operations over the period of "secular stagnation."

What the economy will look like in fifty years is very much a question of the government's proclivities. Will the government choose to step aside and let the private sector roar? Or will the inherently more capable private sector gain the courage of its convictions and quash government? The former scenario is preferable to the latter and will result in more prosperity and well-being. It implies honesty and good character on all counts, whereas the latter does not. If government takes to heart that it is fundamentally irrelevant and envious, it will seek an "altruistic suicide," as French sociologist Émile Durkheim would put it, if not its members' "collective euthanasia–suicide," as German philosopher Karl von Hartmann would put it. This is to speak metaphorically and ontologically. Those participating in the euphemistic "public service" of government will die to their old selves, only to discover their real selves in the burgeoning world-that-is-not-government.

If such an outcome is far-fetched, the wish of dreamers such as Max Stirner and Henry David Thoreau, the other possibility that might result in considerable prosperity would be for the private sector to vanquish the state. It is unlikely, however, that the characterological improvement, process of self-discovery, and recommitment to honesty that are required of all parties for there to be a good society can emerge from the practice of something harsher than the sweet arts of persuasion. Victory typically makes the victors smug and the defeated embittered, both of which are forms of narrow egocentrism and confusion, which cannot be the basis of long-term goods. As Deirdre McCloskey[5] has reminded us, persuasion was a "bourgeois virtue" that replaced the overreliance on the force of arms in the feudal world and was just as effective if not more effective at procuring happy results.

The third option, of course, is for government to continue its petty course and for the private sector to be alternatively complacent about the problem and given to the temptations of regulatory capture. This outcome would be sad, unworthy of the nation perhaps but consistent with Alexis de Tocqueville's concerns about democracy in the America of 175 years ago. It would doom still more millions to careers in government or to the ministration of government mandates in the corporate world—an ocean of wasted lives and human capital. And it would guarantee that prosperity would not come comprehensively because only the private sector can generate prosperity in a mode of self-possession.

Will not technology save us? Peter Thiel perhaps understated the case in his famous remark that at this point in the arc of technological progress, our signature achievement should be something like flying cars, not the ability to type a message in less than 140 characters.[6] Intel, the firm that enabled the personal computer revolution and the Internet, was founded in 1968. Since that year, technological advance has been ungodly, yet the pace of economic growth has been suboptimal, and the American dream has become more elusive, whatever the strivings of the 1980s and 1990s. During the great tech revolution from the 1970s to the 2000s, the government reasserted its ability to get bloated and nosy, overwhelming the gains. Technology cannot save us, just as the tradition of economic growth in this country cannot be reestablished unless government gets ever smaller.

The economist Arthur B. Laffer[7] has summarized the short list of things that can be done to limit government. He refers to the five "pillars of Reaganomics": sound money, low taxes, spare regulation, minimal spending, and free trade. According to the principles of his famous "Laffer curve," the economy will grow so much in a context built on these pillars that government will see expanded receipts and thus have the opportunity to become a fat parasite upon it again. Therefore, the five pillars have to be tried again and again lest the government get large at the expense of the private sector's surpassing wealth. This nation's economy will be a broadly prosperous one in 2065 if the five pillars become the dominant structures of our political economy over the decades up to and including that time. If this happens, our economy will be a historically prosperous one, the most prosperous of all time anywhere, because it was the government's own enlightened decision to become modest.

15

The Future of the Economy

Self-Fulfilling Prophecies

P. J. O'Rourke

WHAT WILL THE economy be like fifty years hence? At a micro-level, for those of us in the age cohort that reads about economics for pleasure, it will be depressed. We'll be dead.

For the living, my prediction is that the economy will be what it is predicted to be. Like all social sciences, economics is a self-fulfilling prophecy.

The idea of a self-fulfilling prophecy has existed at least since the Oedipus myth. The concept was put into formal academic terms in 1949 by Columbia professor Robert K. Merton in his book *Social Theory and Social Structure*.

The self-fulfilling prophecy is in the beginning a *false* definition of the situation that evokes a new behavior that makes the original false conception come *true*. This specious validity of the self-fulfilling prophecy perpetuates a reign of error.

"Reign of error" is as good a definition of economics as any.

Robert K. Merton was the father of modern sociology. He was also the father of Robert C. Merton, who won the Nobel Prize in Economics in 1997 for his work on the Black–Scholes formula—that staple of prediction that calculates futures option pricing for hedge funds. Robert C. Merton was a partner in the Long-Term Capital Management (LTCM) hedge fund, which lost $4.6 billion in 1998.

Not that Robert C.'s predictions didn't come true. He predicted hedge funds could make a lot of money using highly sophisticated mathematical models. All the other hedge funds began using highly sophisticated mathematical models. Some hedge funds made a lot of money. LTCM didn't happen to be one of them.

As the poet Robert Burns put it in "To a Mouse, on Turning Her up in Her Nest with the Plough,"

> But Mousie, thou art no thy lane,
> In proving foresight may be vain:
> The best-laid schemes o' mice an' men Gang aft agley,
> An' lea'e us nought but grief an' pain
> For promis'd joy!
>
> Still thou are blest, compared wi' me!
> The present only toucheth thee:
> But och! I backward cast my e'e,
> On prospects drear!
> An' forward, tho' I canna see,
> I guess an' fear!

I guess and fear our predictions will come true. Humans have remarkable predictive skills. The secret, of course, is to be as vague and obscure as the Delphic Oracle, one of whose prophecies was, "Get out, get out of my sanctum and drown your spirits in woe."

Another expert in vague obscurity was Nostradamus, the sixteenth-century apothecary with a drug store that also dispensed prescriptions for the future. I gather that—if one puts one's mind to it—Nostradamus's abstruse quatrains can be interpreted to foretell everything from the Great Fire of London to the end of the world that we experienced in 2012 due to the expiration of the Mayan calendar.

But we must give the man some credit. In *Les Propheties*, published in 1555, Nostradamus says, "Many rare birds will cry in the air, 'Now! Now!' and sometime later will vanish." Here is Rachel Carson's *Silent Spring* 407 years *avant la lettre*.

Nostradamus also predicted plagues, earthquakes, wars, and floods. Check, check, check, and check. Plus invasion of Europe by Muslims—now a fait accompli, though accomplished by asylum not by assault.

The last book of the Bible, the Revelation of St. John the Divine, is the oldest and most important predictive document of Western civilization. (And, with all respect to the China boom, it's still Western civilization that controls the mind and means of the world's economy.)

But it isn't easy to tell—especially in economic terms—what Revelation is revealing. Is the book allegorical? Yes. "And there appeared a great wonder in heaven; a woman clothed with the sun, and the moon under her feet, and upon her head a crown of twelve stars: And she being with child" (Rev. 12:1–2). This description is clearly symbolic of everything about pregnant celebrities that two millennia later would fill TMZ, E! Online, and all other forms of news media.

Is Revelation admonitory, intended to scare the hell out of us about the future, like the encyclical letter *On Care for Our Common Home* by Pope Francis? Again, yes. Sacrilegious human-induced climate warming resulting from "the wrath of God . . . mingled with fire" causes the polar ice caps to melt, or something. (Apocalypse science is open to criticisms of uncertainty, and its experiments are difficult to replicate.) But, anyway, "every living soul died in the sea" (Rev. 16:3).

Or is the book "a history of the future" meant to be taken literally? Yes, once more. If the current upward trend in consumption of new synthetic hallucinogens such as K2, Spice, and Molly continues, someone will eventually "behold a great red dragon, having seven heads and ten horns" (Rev. 12:3). Back in the 1960s, all we had were regular old hallucinogens, and I saw something with seven heads and ten horns plenty of times in my East Village pad.

As for 666, the "Mark of the Beast" (Rev. 13:18), the Good Book is right again. The numeral 6 is about where your nose is when you're walking down the street with an iPhone pressed to your face but at the same time trying to look out for pedestrians, several of whom you nonetheless bump into, which results in triple 6 snout dials and getting damned to hell by those passersby.

Women over the moon, mass drowning, a dragon that can do the work of an orchestra's entire horn section, and furious people on public sidewalks have, or will have, important economic effects. But as long as humans lived in societies that were mostly agrarian and materially static, economic progress was not the focus of prognostication.

Adam Smith was perhaps the first real economic forecaster. Among Smith's many accurate projections was the abandonment of precious metal coinage in favor of paper money to replace "a very expensive instrument of commerce with one much less costly." He foretold quantitative easing. "The banks, they seem to have thought were in honour bound to supply the deficiency, and to provide them with all the capital which they wanted to trade with." And he worried, too rightly, about what would happen to "the Daedalian wings of paper money" if it became fiat currency untethered to any measure of value.[1] Smith is sometimes faulted for not foreseeing the Industrial Revolution. He didn't foresee it because he knew it was already happening. "Every body must be sensible how much labour is facilitated and abridged by the application of proper machinery. It is unnecessary to give any example."[2] Smith was friends with the inventor of the steam engine, James Watt.

Karl Marx was also, so to speak, on the money. Not about communism, obviously. But that was just a harebrained idea he had. His predictions are another matter. In *The Communist Manifesto,* published in 1848, he showed great prescience, making the call on

> Disappearance of the middle class: Read all about it in each and every Paul Krugman *New York Times* column.
>
> Confiscation of bourgeois property: The IRS called.
>
> Heavy taxation: See above.
>
> Liberation of women: Done.
>
> Dissolution of the nuclear family: Tick that off the list.
>
> Working without material incentive: Have been meaning to talk to my boss about this.
>
> Free public education: And worth it.
>
> Centralization of banking and credit in the hands of the state: Were *you* invited to the last Fed meeting?
>
> Combination of agriculture with manufacturing: How do those factory-farm chicken fingers taste?
>
> Raising the proletariat to the level of the ruling class: See Hillary. See Hillary go.
>
> See Hillary go in the camper van.

Jules Verne wrote *From the Earth to the Moon* in 1865 and *Around the Moon* in 1870. He was wrong about the mechanics of space travel. Shooting Apollo 11 out a cannon wouldn't have worked. But he was right about a Florida blastoff and a Pacific splashdown. And Verne was an absolute visionary concerning the public's socioeconomic attitudes toward lunar travel. He had his own moon-voyaging protagonists express the view that it costs too much and that there's nothing up there, so why bother to go again?

In *Looking Backward: 2000–1887* by Edward Bellamy, published in 1888, the narrator arrives somehow in the year 2000 and is filled in on what's happened in America since Grover Cleveland was elected.

All industries have been subject to nationalization. Or—as we prefer to call it—EPA, NLRB, SEC, FTC, OSHA, EEOC, and Consumer Product Safety Commission regulation.

Delivery of commercial goods is almost instantaneous, in case you thought Jeff Bezos was ahead of his time.

Working hours have been drastically reduced. Bellamy isn't specific about how this was done, but Facebook, Twitter, free porn sites, and computer solitaire in office cubicles have, in fact, reduced working hours to practically zero.

Everyone retires at forty-five. This has not quite happened, but the balance sheets for Social Security and Medicare sure make it look as if it has.

Crime has become a medical issue. That's been true at least since Dan White's "Twinkie defense" during his trial for the murders of San Francisco mayor George Moscone and city supervisor Harvey Milk in 1979.

Plus, according to Bellamy, there's a socialist utopia in America, which we don't have—yet. But not for lack of trying by President Obama.

H. G. Wells was a prolific describer of the future. His novel *The Time Machine* (1895) takes the reader all the way to A.D. 802,701, by which era the blue-collar class and the elites have evolved into different species, the Morlocks and the Eloi.

There was no reason for Wells to jump so far ahead. The Eloi are skinny, vague, naive, entitled, feckless, and childlike. They consider themselves beautiful, do nothing for a living, and eat only fruit. Malibu vegans!

The Morlocks are brutish, apelike troglodytes who know how to make and repair everything, do all the work, and eat Eloi alive. Republicans!

Wells would later adopt what he thought was a more positive attitude to the future. In *Men Like Gods* (1923), 3,000 years of progress have led to peaceful withering of the state—as if we don't have that already, minus the peaceful. A supposedly more advanced race practices telepathy—as if the Internet weren't enough of a sewer dive into the minds of others. And there's no money. What with credit and debit cards and the Daedalian wings of the Federal Reserve, there's hardly any money now. It's not going to take us another 2,908 years before there's none.

In 1933, Wells wrote *The Shape of Things to Come*, a purported history of the world from 1934 to 2016. It is a creepy book. As is often the case in utopian fiction, there's world government. Think of the slaughter and misery caused by little national governments. And futurists want to expand that to planetary size?

But Wells was right in a sense. We'll probably somehow manage to get globalization to do all the damage world government would.

The world government of *The Shape of Things to Come* has repressed all religion—instead of doing what we're doing and just waiting until the last person who still goes to church dies. But we have some holdouts in Muslim lands who are, alas, doing their best to make us see the world government's point.

World government gets rid of religion and nationality, imposes an oligarchy of intellectuals, dictates the rule of "science," enforces English as a universal lingua franca, and does many other things that Wells deems good. All this is accomplished by means of the "Air Police." Drones will suffice.

During the twentieth century, there was, Wells aside, a change in thinking about what the future portended. Predictions went from an optimism that was, sadly, accurate to a pessimism that was accurate, sadly.

Aldous Huxley published *Brave New World* in 1932. The action takes place in the twenty-sixth century. There's that world government again, but at least Huxley had the sense to know it's not a good thing.

Artificial fertilization and fetal genetic manipulation have come a long way from the turkey baster.

Children are bred and conditioned to occupy one of five "castes"—Alfa, Beta, Gamma, Delta, and Epsilon. Call them A-list celebrities, *New York Times* op-ed page columnists, Democratic presidential contenders, people you find on Angie's List to fix the toilet, and members of the NRA. Either that or *Rolling Stone* articles about college fraternity misbehavior are being prefigured.

In this and many other ways, *Brave New World* seems old-fashioned. People in the year 2540 stay youthful until age sixty. Hah! We have octogenarians doing Iron Man triathlons. In the novel, all sex is strictly recreational, but S&M, B&D, LGBT, and Curious sex has not been invented.

Education is conducted by a "hypnopaedic" process. As if school hadn't always put kids to sleep. And the point of this elaborate educational process is to give children subconscious messages about self-esteem. One required reading assignment would have done the trick. Is Maya Angelou's *I Know Why the Caged Bird Sings* out of print in the year 2540 or something?

High art, deep culture, and serious literature no longer exist. Ho-hum. Entertainment deals only with shallow emotions. Same old, same old. People take a drug to make them happy. Big whoop.

In a few remote geographic areas, "savages" are left to their own devices. Thank goodness President Obama got "boots off the ground" in Iraq and Afghanistan.

And George Orwell's *Nineteen Eighty-Four* (1949) is completely antiquated and moss grown.

First, Orwell missed the mark by three decades. The real 1984 was a *bonum anno*. Inflation had been curbed. Unemployment was falling. Gross domestic product growth was 7.3 percent (three times its present rate). Apple introduced its Macintosh personal computer. MacDonald's sold its 50 billionth hamburger. And—"Where's the beef?"—Ronald Reagan was reelected, carrying forty-nine states.

The United States, thanks to a boycott by the Soviet Union, won 174 medals at the Summer Olympics. My Detroit Tigers beat the left-coast loseroid San Diego Padres four to one in the World Series. Hulk Hogan defeated Iron Sheik to become WWF champion. In related news, Iran and Iraq were at war with each other instead of with everybody else in the Middle East. There were nude pictures of Miss America Vanessa Williams. *TV's Bloopers and Practical Jokes* debuted on NBC. And Michael Jackson's hair caught on fire.

But we've caught up with George and surpassed him. WAR IS PEACE-KEEPING. FREEDOM IS SLAVERY REPARATIONS. IGNORANCE IS STRENGTH IN STANDARDIZED TESTING. Three international superstates in perpetual conflict and shifting alliance? We've got four, counting jihadists. *Two* Minutes Hate? Watch *Keeping Up with the Kardashians*. And the telescreen that watches us while we watch it has nothing on the cookies imbedded in that Mac introduced in the real 1984. If you're a man my age, Google anything and watch the Cialis ads pop up.

Our students, teachers, intellectuals, public figures, and even ordinary citizens posting anonymous social media shaming don't need Thought Police because policing thoughts has become a mass DIY project. Examine any history textbook to see the Memory Hole at work on a scale undreamed of by Winston Smith doing his job at the Ministry of Truth and turning former luminaries into unpersons. Sally Hemings is now more revered than Thomas Jefferson. And Orwell's Inner Party comprised 2 percent of the population—grossly inclusive by the standards of our global 1 percent.

The Ministry of Peace is what our Defense Department has been reduced to, if even. The Ministry of Plenty is our entire government. The Ministry of Love is our whole political class; just ask them when they're running for office. And the Ministry of Truth, like the Thought Police, is no longer needed. Its functions have been outsourced to the variously aforementioned *New York Times*.

Will the economics of living and acting and thinking be even worse in 2065 than they are in 2015, let alone in Orwell's 1984? This is up to the self-fulfilling prophecy that is America.

I personally can't imagine a future American who is in any way like me sitting and staring at a "Big Brother Is Watching You" poster with tears streaming down his face for love of Admiral Michael S. Rogers, director of the National Security Agency. But, then again, so far today I haven't had as much to drink as Winston Smith at the end of *Nineteen Eighty-Four*.

16

Through the Mist

American Liberty and Political Economy, 2065

Charlotte A. Twight

ONE CERTAINTY IN writing about America's political economy fifty years hence is that the author will likely be proven wrong. The best one can hope for is to try to appear wise (or at least thoughtful) in the process. Even if the future were determined solely by competitive markets, the outcome would be unknowable. But developments exogenous to private markets will greatly shape the future, making most predictions implicitly or explicitly contingent—impossible to specify in detail without reference to those exogenous events.

A major source of risk and uncertainty that makes predictions contingent is the vast and continuing accretion of discretionary power in America's central state, eroding previous restraints on government authority. Indeed, the U.S. political economy has been so transformed by this accretion of power as to erode any expectation even of stable *constitutional* constraints on government authority. For example, in the U.S. Supreme Court's 2015 decision on the "Affordable Care Act,"[1] the Court undermined our nation's constitutional "*separation of powers*" by rewriting (through reinterpretation) specific language in the congressionally passed Affordable Care Act already signed by the president—clearly a judicial exercise of legislative power. The Court thereby remolded our original countervailing legislative, executive, and judicial powers into seemingly collaborative powers potentially wielded by two to three branches of government in concert.

Another potential exogenous event that poses the risk of nationwide—perhaps civilization-destroying—disablement of our energy infrastructure and incapacitation of motor vehicles is an electromagnetic pulse (EMP), whether caused by an inevitable solar flare or by terrorist/enemy attack using missile-launched, EMP-generating nuclear warheads. Either type of EMP could destroy our unprotected electric power grid and, with it, the lives of most Americans. The power grid is also vulnerable to destruction by direct physical attack on our transformers (a tactic already tested successfully in America by unknown attackers using simple rifles). America's civilization-sustaining electric power grid is thus far more fragile than most Americans imagine.

Despite the uncertainties going forward from unpredictable forces and events exogenous to private markets, broad contours of likely changes to our political economy nonetheless are discernible. I begin with what currently exists: a nominally capitalistic market economy combined with a massive regulatory state having vast internal surveillance capabilities, enormous domestic and international military power, and broad wealth-transfer systems. As a result, government officials now seemingly treat the extent to which private assets and privately produced output remain private as largely a matter of the government's unilateral discretion. The current accumulation of unprecedented government debt and unfunded liabilities, resolvable only by currency debasement and increased taxation, will deprive both private and public sectors of resources throughout the next fifty years, potentially altering the division of resources between them.

In the sections that follow, I briefly survey how the central government acquired and maintains its existing powers and then assess the likelihood of reducing those powers and revitalizing liberty in America.

Establishment of Government Control

Individuals' and businesses' control over their daily economic choices in America is now circumscribed by a vast array of statutory and regulatory powers, many enforced by delegation to state and local officials. Regulations are now so voluminous and unclear that no one can truly know what the rules are, thus eviscerating the "rule of law." For more than a hundred years, these governmental powers have increased unrelentingly, and transaction-cost research applied to governance shows that federal officials have devised sophisticated organizational, regulatory, fiscal, and political tactics to enhance their authority and curtail resistance by the citizenry.

As I have written elsewhere, so enormous is federal authority that there is now "almost no activity that the central government cannot at its discretion regulate, manipulate, or prohibit."[2] Even as America's cherished separation of powers is being eroded, constitutional provisions limiting federal authority to only specifically delegated powers have largely been swept away. In short, the constitutional counterrevolution that began soon after the Constitution's inception accelerated over the past eleven decades, reaching a crescendo in the past twenty years.

In this context, the future of America's political economy will be determined largely by the extent of personal and business autonomy the federal government will tolerate, the additional powers it covets, and the current powers it will not willingly relinquish. The history of federal governance is clear: in deeds and words as well as in law, regulation, and policy, government officials have established the nation-state now defining America, with today's government figuratively sitting astride the activities and work product of the populace. Officials often describe this relationship as a "partnership," ignoring the extent to which it is unilaterally established by force of law.

Financing Government Operations and Constituencies

Today, most Americans readily accept federal extraction, directly and indirectly, of a significant percentage of the value of private production to finance government activities. These activities range from operating the state's constitutionally legitimate system of courts, law enforcement, and national defense to engaging in a vast array of regulatory functions, social service and welfare functions, monetary and fiscal policy activities, land and water resource management, and much more. Complex constituencies have been established through a system of federal contracts, industry regulation, trade policy—including government-to-government deals—preferential tax treatment, subsidies, and grants, thus providing a cornucopia of wealth transfers to those who play the political game.

Dependency as a Means of Social Control

To curtail potential threats to its power and perquisites, the central state has systematically cultivated dependency on the federal government (including dependency by state and local governments). Enormous constituencies have been constructed and nurtured through acquisition of authority over nearly every aspect of human endeavor: education, banking and finance, healthcare, welfare and income redistribution, communications, employer–employee legal relationships, transportation, international trade, the environment, science and technology research and development, energy, retirement income, and beyond.

Dependency is the handmaiden of control, and dependency is the life-blood of modern American governance. To expand its power, the state needed to curtail political resistance and increase political demands for expanded government authority. To that end, the central state honed its manipulation of political transaction costs, raising the costs to citizens of understanding and resisting government actions. This included manipulation of voters' perceptions through long-understood means, such as dispersing and concealing actual costs of government action while concentrating benefits among powerful economic and political interests.

Five decades ahead, what might change the course of this enormous American state and eliminate the existing "dirigisme by indirection"? With education, healthcare delivery, and healthcare financing effectively cartelized and functionally nationalized, and with the majority of the population's old-age financial security largely in the hands of federal bureaucrats, it is hard to envision a majority of the electorate arising—willing to jeopardize their family's education and health or their own financial security in retirement.

In this context, what might resurrect the autonomy of the individual or business enterprise and restore rights of privacy and freedom of contract? What would stimulate the political environment sufficiently to reverse the inertia systematically crafted by the state and its beneficiaries? Moreover, if such a reaction were to materialize, wouldn't most *beneficiaries* of the existing system resist?

Overt and Covert Surveillance: Suppressing Resistance

Surveillance of the citizenry is not new in America. When authorized by legally established probable cause and warrants, it has long been conducted in criminal and intelligence matters. Some extralegal surveillance, especially in military and foreign intelligence operations, also has occurred. But when the Bank Secrecy Act was enacted in 1970—requiring banks to photocopy (and store data on) all checks and mandating government access to that information—legal restraints on surveillance began to diminish. And, of course, since the terrorist attacks on September 11, 2001, searches and surveillance have proliferated, including ubiquitous video surveillance, the groping of travelers at airports, random roadblocks and searches on highways, and wholesale gathering and storage of people's phone calls, email messages, and Internet searches.

To deflect resistance to overt surveillance, federal officials continue to invest in technologies that not only gather and store ever-expanding quantities of individual and business information but also do so using increasingly imperceptible means. Current examples include the National Security Agency's myriad activities, the proliferation of "fusion centers," the creation of the Utah Data Center and other such federal facilities, the deployment of surveillance "pods" like those in Seattle, the use of cameras that record license plate numbers, and the increased government usage of devices such as Stingray to capture cell phone content remotely. Further surveillance and control may soon emerge from the government's rising desire to eliminate the anonymity of cash transactions by requiring all purchases to be made by credit or debit cards.

Over the next fifty years, government's technological capability to surreptitiously monitor the populace and crush domestic dissent or resistance will grow. Use of surveillance and weaponized drones—as well as swarms of drones that function autonomously in accomplishing designated objectives—will become more sophisticated and common in military and law enforcement activities. Unbearable-sound-emitting devices and possible mind-altering technology may become common means of crowd control and suppression of individuals. Equipment that can see through walls and remotely search buildings and vehicles while evading requirements for search warrants will become more common. Face-recognition technology will enable remote identification of people in a crowd by law enforcement and other government officials. Soon, people will never be completely certain that audio and video of their conversations, communication, and behavior are not being recorded or transmitted at any moment in time—whether they are relaxing at home, working, shopping, recreating, or traveling. Imagine the implications of that eventuality for self-censorship and interpersonal (including political) communication.

With these developments in mind, we return to our central question. Given today's vast American administrative state, which future is more likely: that the next fifty years will bring a reduction in the scope of U.S. government power and a corresponding increase in individual liberty or the opposite?

Whichever path the future takes, it will be decided primarily by younger generations of Americans. This fact has long been understood inside and outside of the federal government by those seeking to alter the structure, philosophy, and content of education to serve the interests of the state. Clearly, independent young minds committed to reason and logic, with values *not* inculcated by government, are less predisposed to compliance.

Thus, it is not surprising that over the past century, through federal statutes and regulations and expanding education bureaucracies, government officials have garnered ever-increasing power to shape what children are taught, particularly in their K–12 years. This partially explains why many young adults today don't seem to feel the cost of their lost liberties, liberties their elders knew. For the young, nearly unlimited federal power is the status quo, the norm, something they have been taught to accept without critical analysis. Many have in effect "unlearned" the concept of liberty during their passage through the government education system.

Government Response:
Increasing the Cost of Resistance (Again)

With increasing technological capability for ubiquitous surveillance now inevitable and the tying of healthcare to the central state probably irrevocable, the future cost of resistance to government is almost certain to increase in unanticipated ways. Healthcare likely will soon encompass life-extension and brain-capability-extension technology, both probably under the control of government. Genetic control of aging in a statist system of governance will lead to rationing of its availability and politicization of access. Competition between nations, businesses, universities, and families will drive demand for supplementation of brain capacities through computer-to-brain communication, implantation of electronic supplementation of the human mind, or other means. If these medical technologies are harnessed to further secure the power of America's central government, electronic supplementation of the human brain also is likely to become intimately embedded in government-controlled education, with potential to influence behavior, alter thought processes, and perhaps suppress dissent.

The One Hope?

While a catastrophic economic and political collapse, perhaps resulting from miscalculation and political overreach, might overcome systemic inertia and catalyze renewed demand for liberty, a more likely outcome might be a return to the barbarity of the French Revolution. Perhaps the only change potentially capable of bringing peaceful transformation to a more free society is complete severance of education from government. This change would eliminate the system that has inculcated generations of children in statism and collectivism, reduced children's capacity for reason and logic, and deprived them of lessons of history about the nature of governance and governments' misuse of power.

Is There the Political Will?

How likely is such a severance of education from government control? Government-provided education is mandated in most, if not all, state constitutions, and even government-controlled reforms such as vouchers are bitterly opposed in most states. Parents have learned to love their taxpayer education subsidies and the subsidized child-care system that government schools provide. Teachers, administrators, departments of education, government unions, and companies providing services to them would vehemently resist such change. And the entire apparatus of state, local, and federal government as well as its private-industry beneficiaries would recognize the long-term threat to political and financial control of the populace that totally private education would represent. Independent individuals are a threat to authority. Although autonomous vehicles are being encouraged because they can be tracked, controlled, and shut down, fully autonomous individuals will not be so eagerly embraced.

However, beyond the political interest-group considerations just discussed, might future political support otherwise exist for an education system designed to increase American liberty? Probably not, for liberty itself is a "public good" in an economic sense—nonrival in consumption and nonexcludable. Thus, while costs incurred by those endeavoring to increase liberty will be borne by them personally, the benefits will accrue to all—including those who "free-ride" by trying to get liberty's benefits without taking costly action toward that goal. Even commitment of time to such an endeavor represents opportunity cost, and each individual also will weigh the probability of the effort's success and the risk of retribution by opponents.

In short, whereas free markets are a marvel of voluntary cooperation and productive mutual self-interest, acting for liberty involves collective action and political processes that are subject to the challenges of free-riding incentives described here. Perhaps the only path to creating a widespread free-enterprise education market lies with philosophical commitment by many individuals, foundations, and private schools to outcompeting government schools in the marketplace for education. The market price of private education would need to fall, and the efficiency of delivery and quality of the product must rise to the point where an exodus from government schools occurs. The existence of liberty fifty years hence probably depends on the success of this effort, but economic analysis of political resistance by private interest groups and governments suggests that such freedom is not to be.

17

Conclusion and Final Thoughts

Michael C. Munger

IN THE RESTAURANT *at the End of the Universe* (1980), Douglas Adams says, "To summarize the summary of the summary: people are a problem."[1] I can't offer a better summary, but the papers in this volume offer many perspectives not only on ways "people" are problems but also on ways they are opportunities.

In his essay, Russell D. Roberts reminds us that "software eats the world." And it does. The "world," though, is contingent on a basic truth: transaction costs keep people from eating. If I need my yard raked, why don't I hire the man in Chowmuhani or the man in Ambohitompoina, either of whom would gladly do the work for $5 per day? The answer makes the question seem silly: Chowmuhani is in Bangladesh, and Ambohitompoina is in Madagascar. The costs of finding that willing worker, agreeing on a price, transporting him physically to my leaf-choked yard in Raleigh, North Carolina, and then monitoring his work, dwarfs by several times the mutual gains to be had by what would otherwise be a useful, voluntary transaction. Those three costs—transaction, transport, trust—ensure that the world economy is full of mistakes: resources should move, but they don't.

It doesn't have to be that way. With all respect to Doug Adams (and he's not wrong: people can be a problem!), people are potential assets. Each one of us, on a planet of nearly 7.5 billion people, is underemployed. And that's true of many of the things we own, work with, and see around us but ignore. Markets "move" assets and services toward higher-valued uses; transaction costs keep assets and services locked up.

The reason that "software eats the world" is actually basic economics: factors "want" to be more productive. Of course, that's no truer than saying that giraffes "want" to have long necks. In fact, what is happening is that the relentless search for a surplus leads entrepreneurs to find resources that can be moved, transformed, or combined into products that can be sold at a profit. Transaction costs are a tax that is simply burned, dissipated like the heat from friction in an engine.

One of the themes that recurs in the essays in this volume (including, but certainly not solely, in my own) is that selling reductions in transaction costs can transform the future. In his introduction, Robert M. Whaples rightly tells a history of the modern world in terms of changes in factor productivity. One way of increasing factor productivity is to combine labor with specialized capital and specific knowledge of how to use that capital. In the Industrial Revolution, a steampunk Marc Andreessen might have said, "Division of labor eats the world." And he would have been right. A few workers in Lancashire, England, using Samuel Crompton's "Spinning Mule" could produce far more cloth than hundreds of workers sitting at hand looms. And the cloth was stronger and softer, ensuring that even the poor could afford clothing of a quality that would have been out of the reach of all but the wealthiest elite just half a century earlier. Adam Smith's famous "woolen coat" story presented entrepreneurs' response to increased productivity, which combined division of labor with rapidly evolving innovation in technology. Millions of workers lost their jobs worldwide, not because their jobs were "shipped overseas" but because division of labor eats the world.

The observation that workers would lose their jobs to increased productivity spurred Karl Marx to prophesy that real wages would be driven down and workers ground up on the relentless machinery of ever greater productivity. But the opposite turned out to be the case: prices fell (and have largely continued to fall), and nominal wages rose with productivity. Rising nominal wages and falling prices imply a skyrocketing real wage for much of the world for much of the time since 1750.

But it appears that this central economic fact—consistent, reliably predictable average increases in productivity, widely shared across sectors—may not be eternal. The new value proposition for the production of economic surplus is using software platforms to sell reductions in transaction costs. What are the implications of this change?

That is the question, I think, to which the essays in this volume offer answers. And the answers vary widely. Pierre Lemieux gives a measured answer, with "good polar" and "bad polar" predictions and the likely outcome lying somewhere in between. Most importantly, Lemieux notes that the answer is contingent and identifies three mutually determining factors: the spread of income inequality, Luddite reactions by labor and existing concentrations of function-specific capital, and regulatory policy.

An aggressive regulatory regime, spurred by a "Baptist and bootlegger" coalition of egalitarians and protectionist economic interests, might well slow or derail economic change for decades, with consequent costs to consumers and innovation. An easing of regulatory restrictions or an inability to control an increasingly decentralized and anonymous set of transactions might unleash the zeitgeist of a new age. It all depends on whether Peter J. Boettke's Stupid Horse has the stamina to stay in the race. Our experience with the Stupid Horse is that it is rarely the fastest, but it likewise rarely gets tired or quits.

David R. Henderson offers an array of predictions (and cautions) in his essay and is characteristically modest (and thoughtful). His predictions for increases in "productivity" measure output per worker-hour, but he is careful to note that these effects, including those of mechanization, will result in only modest changes to work hours. Reading between the lines, I expect that Henderson is (plausibly) thinking of the increase in real wages as being in part a product of falling prices, including the myriad services (Facebook, Google, and so on) that are free at the margin to consumers. The basic optimism of the Henderson view is plausible and something worth remembering: although Boettke's Stupid Horse doesn't get tired, it is pretty slow. It takes, as Henderson says, "many barriers" working together in ways that rarely happen to slow innovation or trip up entrepreneurs.

Art Carden and Deirdre N. McCloskey echo Henderson's (and Boettke's) cautious optimism, noting with Adam Smith (in a letter to Sir John Sinclair in 1777) that "there is a great deal of ruin in a nation." They use (as one might expect, considering the source) a most felicitous metaphor—"talk"—for transaction costs. And they likewise capture most beautifully the untapped remaining potential—"enormous productive powers *slumbering in the lap of social labor, led by the bourgeoisie*" (my emphasis)—that reductions in transaction costs might awaken.

Brink Lindsey makes an important point, one that we sometimes forget. Although it is perfectly true that many "goods" in an information economy are free or otherwise unpriced, this probably was even more true in previous epochs. An isolated farm family in southern England and later Iowa likely grew its own crops, made its own furniture, constructed its own dwelling, and raised animals for draft power, milk, and meat. As an economy specializes and division of labor develops, it is true that total output explodes. But it is also true that more products and services pass through the "cash nexus," expanding *measured* gross domestic product (GDP). The difference, as Lindsey notes, is that where economic change once brought things into measured GDP, recent changes may be taking goods and services out of GDP. Nevertheless, productivity can still increase if average workweeks shorten (a common theme among several essays in this collection), and it must be emphasized again that the effect of increases in *real* wages is, if anything, understated by ignoring the unpriced sector: nominal wages may fall sharply, but even a smaller wage goes much further when many valuable services are free.

Of course, to the extent that this effect is pervasive, and if a social safety net offers substitute sustenance, workers may simply drop out of the workforce altogether. The problem—or potential problem, as Lindsey rightly notes—is that the "reservation wage" for many workers who lack substantive skills to work in a knowledge economy may be higher than the wages for jobs they might plausibly attain. Lindsey raises the possibility that this problem might lead to "peak GDP," his version of the Great Stagnation, but he doubts such an event is likely. New electronic products and hardware platforms for enjoying "free" things on the Internet are likely to continue to motivate workers to work and entrepreneurs to hire workers.

Benjamin Powell and Taylor Leland Smith complain about prediction being difficult but do it anyway. Their solution to their "lack of comparative advantage" in predicting the future is then a version of Stein's Law: "If something cannot go on forever, it will stop." Powell and Smith consider several factors—real growth rates of GDP and productivity, changes in economic freedom, growth of deficits, and growth in the "size" of government both in terms of scope and as a proportion of GDP—and conclude that something is going to stop. Their answer is contingent, of course, but if one expects economic freedom to continue to be curtailed and the size of government to continue to expand, then we have seen the end of the kind of economic growth the United States has traditionally expected. That is, the recent decline in U.S. growth rates may appear to coincide with a downturn in the business cycle, but there will be no corresponding prosperity. Powell and Smith do conclude on a (relatively) hopeful note, however, echoing Milton Friedman's famous observation that a crisis is an opportunity for new policies and new directions. The task for those of us who worry about restrictive regulation and rapidly expanding government is to offer alternatives when the crisis comes.

Janet A. Schwartz and Dan Ariely sound a note of caution that not only is plausible, but also downright worrisome. Economic relations and the design of products evolve and adapt much more quickly than human beings' evolved responses to visual, tactile, olfactory, or taste stimuli. In the environment in which we developed, fats, concentrated carbohydrates, and salt were rare but useful to our bodies in terms of energy, electrolyte balance, and survival during periodic famines. There was no problem getting more than enough exercise, so if someone had a chance to sleep all day, that would actually be beneficial rather than harmful.

In short, if a Stone Age human sat down in the shade and found a mound of hot French fries, he would rightly have been pretty excited about eating them all. And that tall frosty 750-calorie cola on the side would have been a bonus. The chance to rest and recover from overused joints and muscles and to accumulate fat and energy might help that hominid survive because next week and the week after that he might have nothing at all to eat except leaves and worms.

The difficulty is that our evolved routines for evaluating things we want to eat and do are now anachronisms. My joints are not overused; I'm already thirty pounds overweight and get hardly any exercise. Yet French fries and sugary drinks still taste just as good and still stimulate the same pleasure centers in my brain that were once adaptive for survival. As leisure and income grow in populations around the world, it is possible to make money—lots of money—by selling people what they want. And modern consumer research and product design can fine-tune products to produce more and more pleasure from experiences in online games (I have seen people play *World of Warcraft* continually for *weeks*), food, drink, and other experiences.

What surprises me is that although Schwartz and Ariely appear to believe (plausibly) that there is a potential problem in matching products to what consumers actually need, they think that these difficulties become advantages when consuming becomes voting. The self-interested corporate employees somehow become benevolent if they are elected to office, and shortsighted consumers somehow recognize their true self-interest at the ballot box. If anything, I would expect the opposite to be true: my vote doesn't determine the outcome of an election; I have no reason to consider alternatives very deeply and no way of obtaining accurate information in the first place. If I know donuts and poutine are bad for me and eat them anyway, what hope do I have to resist the politician who appeals to racially tinged "in-group versus out-group" modules of a brain evolved to live in violent clans of one hundred people who are genetic kin? The problem is much worse for political action than for a commercial setting.

Schwartz and Ariely pose a question: "How much freedom should people have given what *we* know about how *they* really behave . . . ?" (my emphasis). Well, aren't "we" and "they" the same people? Further, one of the things "we know" is that people are even less informed and responsible as voters than they are as consumers. So putting voters in charge of who will regulate consumers is a problem both logically and empirically.

Nevertheless, one has to concede the essential truth of the Schwartz–Ariely challenge: we know for a fact that people will "get it wrong." Increased information and enhanced ability to microtarget may make this problem worse, not better. And just because the solution is not obvious doesn't mean we should pretend the problem doesn't exist. Schwartz and Ariely sound a very useful note of caution, leading us back to Doug Adams's conclusion: "People are a problem."

J. Walker Smith recognizes the potential and some of the pitfalls of the "Uber-All Economy." In particular, he highlights the potential of software platforms to reduce the costs (what I have called "transaction costs") of organizing new markets and new activities. He summarizes the result succinctly but powerfully: all consumer goods will be available as services, and all services will be available on demand. As I note in my own related piece, there is no special reason why so many markets are organized around transaction costs. Uber and Airbnb are perhaps the clearest examples, but it's the nonobvious examples that are the most interesting. Walker offers some provocative speculations about the potential for profound and far-reaching disruptions in the way labor markets and marketing channels are organized. He suggests that there may be fewer, rather than more, effective choices in the future economy, as search algorithms and preference profiles simply deliver what we "want." Still, this scenario should remind us of Alfred North Whitehead's dictum: "Civilization advances by extending the number of important operations which we can perform without thinking about them."[2] The dilemma is that in some sense we *want* choice, but we also benefit when we no longer *have to* choose and get what we want anyway, delivered immediately.

William J. Luther outlines how Bitcoin, or digital exchange-clearing mechanisms, may change the world. There is a debate about whether Bitcoin's key innovation is anonymity or pseudonymous assurance of secure transactions, and I expect the latter will turn out to be more important. The blockchain, regardless of the currency units used to denominate value, is a thunderbolt across the dark sky of nations that lack institutions for clearing transactions. In one step, a transaction system based on Bitcoin can leapfrog the decades-long slog of developing banks, a floating currency, an honest legal system, and an incorruptible police force. Entrepreneurs can work, be productive, and get paid even in lawless failed states such as Somalia and Massachusetts.

L. Lynne Kiesling writes a provocative and entertaining introduction to the "Internet of Things in Your House." The most interesting part of her analysis, which packs many concepts and information into just a few words, is the idea of distributed storage and its implications for entry. Economies of scale and the resulting regulation (justified or not) have precluded entry and have therefore stunted innovation. There may be no Moore's Law for energy innovation, but it is likely that in just a decade or two the nature of the relationship between producer, transmitter, and user will have changed in ways that are difficult to predict. The implications of those changes for the "Internet of Things in Your House" is impossible to foresee. It will be quite a ride!

Brian F. Domitrovic looks ahead fifty years and sees contingency. The performance of the economy will depend substantially on the evolution of government policy and the conception that our governors have of their own role and the function of the state. One possibility, according to Domitrovic, is that the state will "step aside and let the private sector roar," under the apparent assumption (paraphrasing Edmund Burke) that all that is necessary for the triumph of the economy is for bad men to do nothing. Or will "the inherently more capable private sector gain the courage of its convictions and quash government?" This outcome seems implausible because (as Domitrovic himself notes) Mancur Olson's *Logic of Collective Action* indicates that sectoral pressures within business for protection and rent seeking are likely to dominate any encompassing interests of the "private" system. The more likely scenario (as David Henderson also argues in part) is that the state will continue to expand, though not without bounds. The notion of free markets seems to remind even those portions of the business community that rhetorically favor competition of the country song lyrics "Lord, I want to go to Heaven, but I don't want to go tonight!"[3]

P. J. O'Rourke catalogs a substantial portion of the apocalyptically bad history of predictions, including bad predictions regarding the apocalypse itself. His free-verse account of bad prediction would be even funnier if it weren't so accurate. But I found the smile dying on my face as O'Rourke catalogs George Orwell's *correct* predictions regarding Newspeak, Two Minutes Hate, the Memory Hole, and crying at the thought of the beauty and love of the National Security Agency. Jeez, O'Rourke, lighten up a little.

Charlotte Twight's serious essay unintentionally but eerily echoes O'Rourke's catalog of innovations in the use of coercion and centralized planning and control. It seems we stand at a crossroads, and all paths are shrouded in mist, as Twight's title suggests. Will the power of the Internet and decentralized information, energy, and innovation on a global scale reverse the trend toward more state control and scrutiny by those who profess to protect us? Or will *1984* and *Atlas Shrugged* turn out to have been prophetic?

We'll know more in fifty years.

Notes

Chapter 1, Whaples

1. Keynes (1930), 1933, 364.
2. Williamson n.d.
3. Johnston and Williamson 2015.
4. However, Keynes seems to have erred when he suggested that the work week would dwindle to only fifteen hours, a theme explored at length in Pecchi and Piga 2008.
5. Whaples 2006a.
6. The complete set of predictions were: "negative" = 1.4 percent, "zero" = 0 percent, "positive but considerably less than the rate over the past sixty years" = 22.2 percent, "positive but slightly less than the rate over the past sixty years" = 27.8 percent, "about the same as over the past sixty years" = 29.2 percent, "somewhat higher than over the past sixty years" = 16.7 percent, and "considerably higher than over the past sixty years" = 2.8 percent (Whaples 2006a, 279).
7. Palacios-Huerta 2013.
8. Acemoglu 2013, 4, 27.
9. Mas-Colell 2013, 87.
10. Field 2011.
11. See especially table 6.1 in Field's book.
12. Cowen 2013.
13. Gordon 2012, 2.
14. Interviewed in Aeppel 2014. Solow himself is not pessimistic, arguing that "the interval from 1.2 to 1.6 [percentage points] per year is a plausible range of growth" for total factor productivity in the coming century (2013, 138).
15. Rissing et al. 2007, table 2.
16. National Science Foundation 2014, O-6.
17. "Renewable Energy" 2015.
18. Lewis 2015.
19. Gill Pratt discusses the possibilities of a "Cambrian explosion" in robotics, driven by exponential improvements in computing data storage and communications as well as by two "newly blossoming technologies"—"Cloud Robotics" and "Deep Learning"—that "could leverage these base technologies in a virtuous cycle of explosive growth" (2015, 51). He also discusses the key problems in robot capability yet to be solved.
20. Robert Zemeckis 1989.
21. Whaples 2006a, 280–81.
22. Yandle 2016.
23. "Tacitus" n.d.
24. Whaples 2006b, 3.
25. Yankovic 2014.
26. Smith, Son, and Schapiro 2015, 4, 9–10.
27. Documented in Blanchflower and Oswald 2004.
28. Brooks 2015.
29. Or the entire enterprise of using such data in considering public policy may

be fundamentally flawed, as Mark White (2013) argues. Note also that if the income–happiness link depends on relative income, then rising incomes won't increase overall happiness.

30. Lundberg and Pollak 2014.
31. Eberstadt 2015.
32. The argument has been forcefully made that men also benefit immensely from marriage. Marriage appears to cause men's earnings to rise because it gives them a new sense of meaning and a stronger incentive to become economically productive; it also appears to substantially reduce mortality rates for men (see Schwartz 2005).
33. Schwartz 2005.
34. Wilcox and Lerman 2014, 17.
35. Marshall and Hederman 2014, 22.
36. Eberstadt 2015.
37. Ibid.
38. Among the vast research on the causes of declining fertility, note two interesting studies. First, Eli Berman, Laurence Iannaccone, and Giuseppe Ragusa (2012) find that in Catholic European countries the decline in fertility has been driven in part by an earlier drop in church attendance and professions to religious life. Declining church attendance could cause a shift toward desiring material possessions rather than children, and the decrease in the number professed to religious life (for example, as teachers in parochial schools) may indicate a decline in church-related support for children. If this trend also holds for the United States, it suggests that the total U.S. fertility rate may continue to decline as church attendance continues to erode (see Gray 2011), with the portion of those who never or rarely attend church rising from 29 percent in 1972 to 43 percent in 2012 (Marshall and Hederman 2014, 28). Second, Michael Malcolm

and George S. Naufal (forthcoming) argue that Internet pornography and marriage are substitutes. I hesitate to introduce this issue, but if pornography is a substitute for personal relationships and marriage, the development of increasingly lifelike sex robots might have a profound impact within the next fifty years. And the lure of substitution may be strong for women, too. For example, Molly McHugh opines that, "[n]aturally, something we've long wanted to task robots with is sex" and then details breakthroughs in robosex technology (2015).

39. Sacks 2015, 14–15.
40. Budziszewski 2014.
41. See Higgs (1987) 2013.

Chapter 2, Lemieux

1. Sabin 2013.
2. Keynes (1930) 1963.
3. CBO 2014.
4. See Lemieux 2014.
5. Lemieux 2014–15.
6. Murray 2015.
7. Lemieux 2014–15 and references cited therein.
8. Lemieux 2014–15.
9. Tocqueville (1840) 2010, 1251–53.
10. Hummel 2011.
11. Kain 2011.
12. This idea has been circulating in academic circles for a few decades; see Lemieux 2015.
13. Lemieux 2014.
14. Murray 2015.
15. National Intelligence Council 2012.
16. Kahn and Wiener 1967.
17. Keynes (1930) 1963; Kahn and Wiener 1967.
18. Murray 2015.
19. Lemieux 2013.
20. Buchanan 2005.
21. Shannon et al. n.d.

Chapter 3, Boettke

1. Simon 1983.
2. Smith (1776) 1976, book 4, chap. 5, 49–50.

Chapter 4, Henderson

1. Rae 1895.
2. Larry Jones, Alice Schoonbroodt, and Michele Tertilt (2008) address the problems with this theory.
3. Jones, Schoonbroodt, and Tertilt 2008, 6.
4. World Bank 2015b, 1.
5. World Bank 2015a.
6. For an excellent discussion of the market forces that keep prices of fuels and minerals from rising substantially and even cause them to fall, see Blackman and Baumol 2008.
7. Ausubel 2015.
8. Henderson and Hummel 2014.
9. Gwartney, Lawson, and Hall 2014.

Chapter 5, Carden and McCloskey

1. Tetlock 2006.
2. Asimov 1951.
3. McCloskey 2006, 2010, 2016.
4. Gordon 2012.
5. Cowen 2013.
6. See Piketty 2014.
7. Sun Tzu [1910].
8. Gerschenkron 1971, 655.
9. Ridley 2010.

Chapter 6, Lindsey

1. Gordon 2012.
2. Summers 2014.
3. Murphy and Topel 2006, 891.
4. Lindsey 2013, fig. 2
5. Ibid. table 3.
6. Fogel 2004, table 4.4.

7. Francis 2006.
8. Shirky 2010.
9. See, e.g., "Onrushing Wave" 2014; Ford 2015.
10. The calculations I present use the Personal Consumption Expenditures price index to adjust for inflation. The Consumer Price Index is more commonly used to adjust for inflation, but it is widely believed to overstate inflation and thus to understate growth in real wages.
11. Juhn and Potter 2006, table 3.
12. Duggan 2015.
13. U.S. Bureau of Labor Statistics 2014, table 8.

Chapter 7, Roberts

1. Gordon 2012.
2. Andreessen 2011.

Chapter 8, Powell and Smith

1. Business Cycle Dating Committee 2010.
2. U.S. Bureau of Economic Analysis 2015.
3. U.S. Bureau of Labor Statistics 2015.
4. Ibid.
5. U.S. Bureau of Economic Analysis 2015.
6. The U.S. Bureau of Labor Statistics (2015) defines *labor force* as the civilian noninstitutional population older than sixteen.
7. Gwartney, Lawson, and Hall 2014.
8. Ironically, the U.S. score for sound money has not declined significantly (9.7 in 2008 to 9.3 in 2012) despite various Federal Reserve measures, including "quantitative easing," because the index uses a measure of price inflation that does not reflect the magnitude of Fed money creation; much of the

increased money supply has merely become excess bank reserves (Gwartney, Lawson, and Hall n.d.).

9. U.S. Bureau of Economic Analysis 2015.

10. Gwartney, Lawson, and Hall 2014.

11. *Kelo v. City of New London*, 545 U.S. 469 (2005).

12. As James Sherk and Todd Zywicki point out, during the bailout of General Motors and Chrysler, the Obama administration effectively subsidized United Auto Workers (UAW) compensation at the taxpayers' expense and offered preferential treatment to the UAW over other bankruptcy creditors. "Legally the UAW's claims had the same status as those of other unsecured creditors, but the UAW recovered a much greater proportion of the debts that General Motors and Chrysler owed the union" (2012).

13. Hall and Lawson 2014.

14. Gwartney, Lawson, and Holcombe 1999.

15. CBO 2014.

16. Greece, for example, has a debt-to-GDP ratio of 175 percent (Kotlikoff 2015).

17. Kotlikoff 2015, 5.

18. Gokhale 2014, 67–98.

19. Nowrasteh 2015.

20. Kotlikoff 2015, 5

21. Hummel 2015.

22. U.S. Congressional Budget Office 2013.

23. U.S. Congressional Budget Office 2011.

24. Jeffrey Hummel (2015; Henderson and Hummel 2014) argues that the U.S. government is headed to a default and repudiation of its debt. In addition, he advocates this outcome as his favored solution to the current fiscal imbalance.

25. Friedman (1962) 2002, xiv.

26. Although this scenario would improve the economy in the future, it would not cure the unfunded liabilities and debt that cause the crisis. Some form of default, repudiation, or benefits cuts would still have to occur. See Hummel 2015 for an argument that default and repudiation of debt are morally superior to cutting Social Security or Medicare obligations.

Chapter 9, Schwartz and Ariely

1. Reproduced with permission of Metro Trains.

Chapter 10, Smith

1. Miessler 2015.

2. Frey and Osborne 2013.

3. Ibid.

4. Cowen 2013.

Chapter 11, Munger

1. Clark 2014.

2. Diamond 1987.

3. See Hummel 2012 for background.

4. Smith (1776/1904) 1981.

5. Lucas 1979; Langlois 1992.

Chapter 12, Luther

1. Shasky Calvery 2013.

2. Taleb 2013.

3. Krugman 2014.

4. Luther forthcoming.

5. Luther and White 2014 considers recent attempts to reduce the costs of switching. Still, switching costs are positive. See also Luther 2014.

6. Luther and White 2011; Luther forthcoming.

7. Nair and Cachanosky 2014 discusses entrepreneurial efforts to overcome these network effects.

8. On the role of government in determining the medium of exchange, see Salter and Luther 2014.

9. Luther 2015.
10. Hendrickson, Hogan, and Luther forthcoming.
11. Grinberg 2011, 182.
12. For a more comprehensive overview of the market for cryptocurrencies, see White 2015.
13. At the time of this writing, the website Crypto-Currency Market Capitalizations (http://coinmarketcap.com/all/views/all/) tracked 680 cryptocurrencies, of which 580 had a positive value. All market capitalization data presented herein come from this source.
14. White 2015, 384.
15. Specifically, custodians maintain constant sell walls at U.S.$1.00, and shareholders offer interest on NuBits effectively held out of circulation to create synthetic demand when necessary. Since launching in September 2014, NuBits's price has ranged from a low of $0.94 in May 2015 to a high of $1.06 in February 15.
16. Nora Ephron 1998.
17. Luther and Olson 2015 compares the blockchain to memory.
18. Orcutt 2015.
19. Rizzo 2015.
20. U.S. Federal Reserve System 2015.
21. Christin 2013.
22. Hajdarbegovic 2014.
23. Luther 2013, forthcoming.
24. Burns 2015.

Chapter 13, Kiesling

1. Whitehead 1911, 46.
2. Hayek 1960, 26.
3. Smil 2015.
4. Thierer 2014.
5. Kiesling 2014.

Chapter 14, Domitrovic

1. Jenkins 2012.
2. Harrington 1962.
3. Furman 2013.
4. See Kudlow and Domitrovic forthcoming.
5. McCloskey 2006.
6. Packer 2011.
7. Domitrovic 2014.

Chapter 15, O'Rourke

1. Smith (1776/1976) 1981, 292, 308, 321.
2. Ibid. 19.

Chapter 16, Twight

1. *King v. Burwell*, 576 U.S. (2015).
2. Twight 2002, back cover.

Chapter 17, Munger

1. Adams (1980) 1995, 197.
2. Whitehead 1911, 46.
3. Diffie 1993.

Glossary

Bitcoin   A type of digital currency, created in 2009, in which encryption techniques are used to regulate the generation of units of currency and verify the transfer of funds. The world's first global currency, which operates independently of any central bank and relies completely on free market processes.

Blockchain   A public ledger where bitcoin transactions are recorded and confirmed anonymously.

Cash nexus   Human interactions that are governed by the exchange of money.
- A relationship between people that is based on the exchange of money (e.g. the employer-employee relationship).
- Interactions between people done entirely for monetary reasons.

Division of Labor   The assignment of different parts of a production process to different people in order to improve efficiency and reduce the cost of production.
- The specialization of a worker's tasks to increase the efficiency of production (e.g. an assembly line).

Economies of scale   Reductions in the cost of producing a unit of a good that arise from producing on a larger scale.
- The inverse relationship between the amount of a good produced and the average cost of producing each unit.

Function-specific capital   Capital goods (money, machinery, etc.) that can be used only for producing a specific consumer good.

Income inequality   The range of income differences within or across populations.

Measured GDP   The market value of the final goods and services produced within an economy in a year (as measured in the U.S. by the Bureau of Economic Analysis).

Moore's Law   The observation that, over the history of computing hardware, the number of transistors in a dense integrated circuit has doubled approximately every two years.

Peak GDP   The highest Gross Domestic Product that a country attains during the course of its development.

Rent-seeking   Lobbying for special treatment by the government to create economic profit or divert gains away from others.

Reservation wage   The lowest wage at which an individual is willing to work.

Search algorithm   A formula used to retrieve specific information among a collection of information.

Total Factor Productivity   A measure of the ability to turn inputs (e.g. labor, capital, raw materials) into output.

Transaction cost   The costs of making and enforcing the terms of an economic exchange.

References

Acemoglu, Daron. 2013. The World Our Grandchildren Will Inherit. In *In 100 Years: Leading Economists Predict the Future,* edited by Ignacio Palacios-Huerta, 1–35. Cambridge, Mass.: MIT Press.

Adams, Douglas. (1980) 1995. *The Restaurant at the End of the Universe.* Reprint, New York: Del Rey.

Aeppel, Timothy. 2014. Economists Debate: Has All the Important Stuff Already Been Invented? *Wall Street Journal,* June 15. At http://www.wsj.com/articles/economists-duel-over-idea-that-technology-will-save-the-world-1402886301.

Andreessen, Marc. 2011. Why Software Is Eating the World. *Wall Street Journal,* August 20.

Asimov, Isaac. 1951. *Foundation.* New York: Gnome Press.

Ausubel, Jesse H. 2015. Nature Rebounds. Paper presented at the Long Now Foundation Seminar, San Francisco, January 13. At http://phe.rockefeller.edu/docs/Nature_ Rebounds.pdf.

Bellamy, Edward. 1888. *Looking Backward: 2000–1887.* New York: Houghton Mifflin. Huxley, Aldous. 1932. *Brave New World.* London: Chatto & Windus.

Berman, Eli, Laurence Iannaccone, and Giuseppe Ragusa. 2012. *From Empty Pews to Empty Cradles: Fertility Decline among European Catholics.* Working Paper no. 18350. Cambridge, Mass.: National Bureau of Economic Research.

Blackman, Sue Anne Batey, and William J. Baumol. 2008. Natural Resources. In *The Concise Encyclopedia of Economics,* edited by David R. Henderson. Indianapolis, Ind.: Liberty Fund. At http://www.econlib.org/library/Enc/NaturalResources.html.

Blanchflower, David G., and Andrew J. Oswald. 2004. Well-Being over Time in Britain and the USA. *Journal of Public Economics* 88, nos. 7–8: 1359–86.

Brooks, Arthur. 2015. *The Conservative Heart: How to Build a Fairer, Happier, and More Prosperous America.* New York: Broadside Books.

Buchanan, James M. 2005. Afraid to Be Free: Dependency as Desideratum. *Public Choice* 124:19–31.

Budziszewski, J. 2014. Fragment from an Earlier Civilization. At http://www.under groundthomist.org/fragment-from-an-earlier-civilization.

Burns, Scott. 2015. Mobile Money and Financial Development: The Case of M-pesa in Kenya. Early draft of unpublished working paper in author's files.

Business Cycle Dating Committee, National Bureau of Economic Research. 2010. *The Business Cycle Dating Committee September Report.* Cambridge, Mass.: National Bureau of Economic Research. At http://www.nber.org/cycles/sept2010 .html.

Calvery, Jennifer Shasky. 2013. Testimony. In U.S. Senate, Committee on Homeland Security and Government Affairs, *Digital Currencies,* hearings, 113th Cong., 1st sess., November 18.

Christin, Nicolas. 2013. Traveling the Silk Road: A Measurement Analysis of a Large Anonymous Online Marketplace. In *WWW '13: Proceedings of the 22nd International Conference on World Wide Web,* 213–23. Geneva: International World Wide Web Conferences Steering Committee.

Clark, Patrick. 2014. Hoarder Nation: America's Self-Storage Industry Is Booming. *Bloomberg News,* December 1. At http://www.bloomberg.com/bw/articles/ 2014-12-01/cyber- monday-gifts-final-resting-place-self-storage.

Cowen, Tyler. 2013. *Average Is Over: Powering America beyond the Age of the Great Stagnation.* New York: Dutton.

Diamandis, Peter H., and Steven Kotler. 2012. *Abundance: The Future Is Better Than You Think.* New York: Free Press.

Diamond, Jared. 1987. The Worst Mistake in the History of the Human Race. *Discover,* May, 64–66.

Diffie, Joe. "Prop Me Up Beside the Jukebox (If I Die)." On *Honky Tonk Attitude* (album). Epic Records, 1993.

Domitrovic, Brian, ed. 2014. *The Pillars of Reaganomics: A Generation of Wisdom from Arthur Laffer and the Supply-Side Revolutionaries.* San Francisco: Pacific Research Institute.

Duggan, Mark G. 2015. Testimony. In U.S. Senate, Committee on the Budget, *The Coming Crisis: Social Security Disability Trust Fund Insolvency,* hearings, 112th Cong., 1st sess., February 11.

Eberstadt, Nicholas. 2015. The Global Flight from the Family. *Wall Street Journal,* February 20.

Field, Alexander J. 2011. *A Great Leap Forward: 1930s Depression and U.S. Economic Growth.* New Haven, Conn.: Yale University Press.

Fogel, Robert William. 2004. *The Escape from Hunger and Premature Death, 1700– 2100: Europe, America, and the Third World.* New York: Cambridge University Press.

Ford, Martin. 2015. *Rise of the Robots: Technology and the Threat of a Jobless Future.* New York: Basic Books.

Francis, David R. 2006. Why High Earners Work Longer Hours. *NBER Digest,* July. At http://www.nber.org/digest/jul06/w11895.html.

Frey, Carl Benedikt, and Michael Osborne. 2013. *The Future of Employment: How Susceptible Are Jobs to Computerisation?* Oxford: Oxford Martin School, Programme on the Impacts of Future Technology and Programme on Technology and Employment, Oxford University, September 17. At http://www.oxfordmartin.ox .ac.uk/downloads/academic/The_Future_ of_Employment.pdf.

Friedman, Milton. 2002. *Capitalism and Freedom.* Chicago: University of Chicago Press.

Furman, Jason. 2013. Testimony. In U.S. House of Representatives and Senate, Joint Economic Committee, *The Economic Outlook,* hearings, 113th Cong., 1st sess., November 13.

Gerschenkron, Alexander. 1971. Mercator Gloriosus: Review of John Hicks's *Theory of Economic History. Economic History Review* 24:653–66.

Gokhale, Jagadeesh. 2014. *The Government Debt Iceberg.* Research Monograph no. 68. London: Institute of Economic Affairs.

Gordon, Robert. 2012. *Is U.S. Economic Growth Over? Faltering Innovation Confronts the Six Headwinds.* Working Paper no. 18315. Cambridge, Mass.: National Bureau of Economic Research.

Gray, Mark M. 2011. Sunday Morning: Deconstructing Catholic Mass Attendance in the 1950s and Now. At http://nineteensixty-four.blogspot.com/2011/03/sunday -morning- deconstructing-catholic.html.

Grinberg, Reuben. 2011. Bitcoin: An Innovative Alternative Digital Currency. *Hastings Science & Technology Law Journal* 4, no. 1: 159–208.

Gwartney, James, Robert Lawson, and Joshua Hall. 2014. *Economic Freedom of the World, 2014.* Vancouver: Fraser Institute.

——————. 2015. *Economic Freedom of the World: 2015 Annual Report.* Vancouver: Fraser Institute. At http://www.fraserinstitute.org and http://www.freetheworld.com.

——————. n.d. *Economic Freedom of the World Index.* At http://www.efwdata.com. Accessed October 13, 2015.

Gwartney, James D., Robert A. Lawson, and Randall G. Holcombe. 1999. Economic Freedom and the Environment for Economic Growth. *Journal of Institutional and Theoretical Economics* 155, no. 4: 643–63.

Hajdarbegovic, Nermin. 2014. Facebook Approves First Cryptocurrency Tipping Apps. *CoinDesk,* June 6.

Hall, Joshua C., and Robert A. Lawson. 2014. Economic Freedom of the World: An Accounting of the Literature. *Contemporary Economic Policy* 32, no. 1: 1–19.

Harrington, Michael. 1962. *The Other America: Poverty in the United States*. New York: Macmillan.

Hayek, F. A. 1960. *The Constitution of Liberty*. Chicago: University of Chicago Press.

Henderson, David, and Jeffery Rogers Hummel. 2014. The Inevitability of a U.S. Government Default. *The Independent Review* 18, no. 4 (Spring): 527–41.

Hendrickson, Joshua R., Thomas L. Hogan, and William J. Luther. Forthcoming. The Political Economy of Bitcoin. *Economic Inquiry.*

Higgs, Robert. [1987] 2013. *Crisis and Leviathan: Critical Episodes in the Growth of American Government.* Oakland, Calif.: Independent Institute.

Hummel, Jeffrey Rogers. 2011. Ben Bernanke versus Milton Friedman: The Federal Reserve's Emergence as the U.S. Economy's Central Planner. *The Independent Review* 15, no. 4 (Spring): 485–518.

——————. 2012. The Will to Be Free: The Role of Ideology in National Defense. *Mises Circle Features,* December 9. At http://themisescircle.org/features/the- will -to-be-free/.

——————. 2015. The Consequences of a United States Default or Repudiation. In *Aftermath: What Happens after the Crisis?* edited by Steven Balch and Benjamin Powell, 157–201. Lubbock: Free Market Institute, Texas Tech University.

Huxley, Aldous. 1932. *Brave New World*. London: Chatto & Windus.

Issues in Science and Technology 23, no. 3. At http://issues.org/23-3/wadhwa/.

Jenkins, Holman. 2012. GM Faces Its Own Regulatory Cliff. *Wall Street Journal*, August 22.

Johnston, Louis, and Samuel H. Williamson. 2015. What Was the U.S. GDP Then?

Jones, Larry E., Alice Schoonbroodt, and Michele Tertilt. 2008. *Fertility Theories: Can They Explain the Negative Fertility–Income Relationship?* Working Paper no. 14266. Cambridge, Mass.: National Bureau of Economic Research, August.

Juhn, Chinhui, and Simon Potter. 2006. Changes in Labor Force Participation in the United States. *Journal of Economic Perspectives* 20, no. 3: 27–46.

Kahn, Herman, and Anthony J. Wiener. 1967. *The Year 2000. A Framework for Speculation on the Next Thirty-Three Years.* New York: Macmillan.

Kain, Erik. 2011. The Inexplicable War on Lemonade Stands. *Forbes*, August 3. At http:// www.forbes.com/sites/erikkain/2011/08/03/the-inexplicable-war-on -lemonade-stands/.

Kelo v. City of New London, 545 U.S. 469 (2005).

Keynes, John Maynard. [1930] 1963. Economic Possibilities for Our Grandchildren. In *Essays in Persuasion*, 358–73. New York: Norton, 1963.

——————. [1930] 1933. *Economic Possibilities for Our Grandchildren*. In *Essays in Persuasion*, 358–65. London: Macmillan.

Kiesling, Lynne. 2014. Incumbent Vertical Market Power, Experimentation, and Institutional Design in the Deregulating Electricity Industry. *The Independent Review* 19, no. 2 (Fall): 239–64.

King v. Burwell, 576 U.S. (2015).

Kotlikoff, Lawrence J. 2015. America's Fiscal Insolvency and Its Generational Consequences. Testimony in U.S. Senate, Budget Committee, *The Coming Crisis: America's Dangerous Debt*, hearings, 114th Cong., 1st sess., February 25.

Krugman, Paul. 2014. The Long Cryptocon: The Conscience of a Liberal. *New York Times*, October 4.

Kudlow, Larry, and Brian Domitrovic. Forthcoming. *JFK and the Reagan Revolution: A Secret History of American Prosperity*. New York: Penguin Sentinel.

Langlois, Richard. 1992. Transactions Cost Economics in Real Time. *Industrial and Corporate Change* 1:99–127.

Lemieux, Pierre. 2013. *The Public Debt Problem*. New York: Macmillan.

————. 2014. *Who Needs Jobs? Spreading Poverty or Increasing Welfare*. New York: Palgrave Macmillan.

————. 2014–15. A Slow-Motion Collapse. *Regulation* 37, no. 4: 12–15.

————. 2015. The Dangers of "Public Health." *Regulation* 38, no. 3 (Fall): 30–35.

Lewis, John S. 2014. *Asteroid Mining 101: Wealth for the New Space Economy*. Moffett Field, Calif.: Deep Space Industries.

Lindsey, Brink. 2013. *Why Growth Is Getting Harder*. Policy Analysis no. 737. Washington, D.C.: Cato Institute.

Lucas, Robert. 1979. Sharing, Monitoring, and Incentives: Marshallian Misallocation Reassessed. *Journal of Political Economy* 87, no. 3: 501–21.

Lundberg, Shelly, and Robert A. Pollak. 2014. Cohabitation and the Uneven Retreat from Marriage in the U.S., 1950–2010. In *Human Capital in History: The American Record*, edited by Leah Platt Boustan, Carola Frydman, and Robert A. Margo, 241–72. Chicago: University of Chicago Press.

Luther, William J. 2013. Friedman versus Hayek on Private Outside Monies: New Evidence for the Debate. *Economic Affairs* 33, no. 1: 127–35.

————. 2014. Will Bitcoin Survive? *Kenyon College Alumni Bulletin* 36, no. 4: 36.

————. 2015. Regulating Bitcoin: On What Grounds? Unpublished working paper. At http://papers.ssrn.com/sol3/papers.cfm?abstract_id=2631307.

————. Forthcoming. Cryptocurrencies, Network Effects, and Switching Costs. *Contemporary Economic Policy*.

Luther, William J., and Josiah Olson. 2015. Bitcoin Is Memory. *Journal of Prices & Markets* 3, no. 3: 22–33.

Luther, William J., and Lawrence H. White. 2011. *Positively Valued Fiat Money after the Sovereign Disappears: The Case of Somalia*. Working Paper in Economics no. 11-14. Fairfax, Va.: George Mason University.

_____. 2014. Can Bitcoin Become a Major Currency? *Cayman Financial Review* 36:78–79.

Malcolm, Michael, and George S. Naufal. Forthcoming. Are Pornography and Marriage Substitutes for Young Men? *Eastern Economic Journal.* At http://www .palgrave-journals.com/eej/ journal/vaop/ncurrent/full/eej20157a.html.

Marshall, Jennifer A., and Rea S. Hederman. 2014. *2014 Index of Culture and Opportunity: The Social and Economic Trends That Shape America.* Washington, D.C.: Heritage Foundation.

Marx, Karl. 1848. *The Communist Manifesto.* London: Workers Educational Association. Merton, Robert K. 1949. *Social Theory and Social Structure.* New York: Free Press.

Mas-Colell, Andreu. 2013. Keynes, His Grandchildren, and Ours. In *In 100 Years: Leading Economists Predict the Future,* edited by Ignacio Palacios-Huerta, 85–97. Cambridge, Mass.: MIT Press.

McCloskey, Deirdre N. 2006. *The Bourgeois Virtues: Ethics for an Age of Commerce.* Chicago: University of Chicago Press.

_____. 2010. *Bourgeois Dignity: Why Economics Can't Explain the Modern World.* Chicago: University of Chicago Press.

_____. 2016. *Bourgeois Equality: How Ideas, Not Capital or Institutions, Enriched the World.* Chicago: University of Chicago Press.

McHugh, Molly. 2015. Sex and Love in the Age of Robots. *The Kernel,* February 8. At http:// kernelmag.dailydot.com/issue-sections/features-issue-sections/11649/ sex-robot-future- roxxxxy/.

MeasuringWorth. At http://www.measuringworth.org/usgdp/.

Metro Trains. "Dumb Ways to Die." Performed by Tangerine Kitty. Lyrics by John Mescall. Music by Ollie McGill. Vocals by Emily Lubitz.

Miessler, Daniel. 2015. The Real Internet of Things. Blog, May 9. At https://daniel miessler.com/blog/real-internet-of-things/.

Murphy, Kevin M., and Robert H. Topel. 2006. *The Value of Health and Longevity.* Working Paper no. 11405. Cambridge, Mass.: National Bureau of Economic Research.

Murray, Charles. 2015. *By the People: Rebuilding Liberty Without Permission.* New York: Crown Forum.

Nair, Malavika, and Nicolas Cachanosky. 2014. Entrepreneurship and Bitcoin: Breaking the Network Effect. Early draft of unpublished working paper in author's files.

Nakamoto, Satoshi. 2008. Bitcoin: A Peer-to-Peer Electronic Cash System. Unpublished working paper. At https://bitcoin.org/bitcoin.pdf.

National Intelligence Council (NIC). 2012. *Global Trends 2030: Alternative Worlds.* Washington, D.C.: National Intelligence Council. At http://www.dni.gov/index .php/about/organization/ global-trends-2030.

National Science Foundation. 2014. *Science and Engineering Indicators, 2014: Overview.* Washington, D.C.: National Science Foundation.

Nowrasteh, Alex. 2015. The Fiscal Impact of Immigration. In *The Economics of Immigration,* edited by Benjamin Powell, 38–69. New York: Oxford University Press.

Olson, Mancur. 1965. *The Logic of Collective Action: Public Goods and the Theory of Groups.* Cambridge, Mass.: Harvard University Press.

The Onrushing Wave. 2014. *Economist,* June 18.

Orcutt, Mike. 2015. Why Nasdaq Is Betting on Bitcoin's Blockchain. *MIT Technology Review,* July 9, n.p.

Orwell, George. 1949. *Nineteen Eighty-Four.* London: Secker & Warburg.

Packer, George. 2011. No Death, No Taxes. *New Yorker,* November 28.

Palacios-Huerta, Ignacio, ed. 2013. *In 100 Years: Leading Economists Predict the Future.* Cambridge, Mass.: MIT Press.

Pecchi, Lorenzo, and Gustavo Piga. 2008. *Revisiting Keynes: Economic Possibilities for our Grandchildren.* Cambridge, Mass.: MIT Press.

Piketty, Thomas. 2014. *Capital in the Twenty-First Century.* Translated by Arthur Goldhammer. Cambridge, Mass.: Harvard University Press.

Pratt, Gill A. 2015. Is a Cambrian Explosion Coming for Robotics? *Journal of Economic Perspectives* 29, no. 3: 51–60.

Rae, John. 1895. *Life of Adam Smith.* London: Macmillan.

Renewable Energy: Not a Toy. Plummeting Prices Are Boosting Renewables, Even as Subsidies Fall. 2015. *Economist,* April 11. At http://www.economist.com/news/international/ 21647975-plummeting-prices-are-boosting-renewables-even-subsidies-fall-not-toy.

Ridley, Matt. 2010. *The Rational Optimist: How Prosperity Evolves.* New York: Harper.

Rissing, Ben, Gary Gereffi, Ryan Ong, and Vivek Wadhwa. 2007. Where the Engineers Are. *Issues in Science and Technology* 23, no. 3. At http://issues.org/23-3/wadhwa/.

Rizzo, Pete. 2015. Deloitte Trials Blockchain Tech for Client Auditing. *CoinDesk,* July 14.

Sabin, Paul. 2013. *The Bet: Paul Ehrlich, Julian Simon, and Our Gamble over Earth's Future.* New Haven, Conn.: Yale University Press.

Sacks, Jonathan. 2015. The Love That Brings New Life into the World. *Columbia* 95, no. 5: 12–15.

Salter, Alexander W., and William J. Luther. 2014. Synthesizing State and Spontaneous Order Theories of Money. *Advances in Austrian Economics* 18:161–78.

Schwartz, Joel. 2005. The Socio-economic Benefits of Marriage: A Review of Recent Evidence from the United States. *Economic Affairs* 25, no. 3: 45–51.

Shannon, Sarah, Christopher Uggen, Melissa Thompson, Jason Schnittker, and Michael Massoglia. n.d. Growth in the U.S. Ex-felon and Ex-prisoner Population, 1948–2010. At http://paa2011.princeton.edu/papers/111687. Accessed September 6, 2015.

Sherk, James, and Todd Zywicki. 2012. *Auto Bailout or UAW Bailout? Taxpayer Losses Came from Subsidizing Union Compensation.* Backgrounder no. 2700. Washington, D.C.: Heritage Foundation. At http://www.heritage.org/research/reports/2012/06/auto-bailout-or-uaw-bailout-taxpayer-losses-came-from-subsidizing-union-compensation.

Shirky, Clay. 2010. *Cognitive Surplus: How Technology Makes Consumers into Collaborators.* New York: Penguin Press.

Simon, Julian. 1983. *The Ultimate Resource.* Princeton, N.J.: Princeton University Press.

Smil, Vaclav. 2015. Moore's Curse. *IEEE Spectrum,* March 19. At http://spectrum.ieee.org/ energy/renewables/moores-curse.

Smith, Adam. [1776] 1976. *An Inquiry into the Nature and Causes of the Wealth of Nations.* Chicago: University of Chicago Press.

_____. [1776/1976] 1981. *An Inquiry into the Nature and Causes of the Wealth of Nations.* Edited by R. H. Campbell and A. S. Skinner. Oxford: Oxford University Press. Reprint, Indianapolis, Ind.: Liberty Fund.

_____. [1776/1904] 1981. *An Inquiry into the Nature and Causes of the Wealth of Nations.* Edited with an introduction, notes, marginal summary, and an enlarged index by Edwin Cannan. London: Methuen. Reprint, Indianapolis, Ind.: Liberty Fund.

Smith, Tom W., Jaesok Son, and Benjamin Schapiro. 2015. *General Social Survey Final Report: Trends in Psychological Well-Being, 1972–2014.* Chicago: National Opinion Research Center.

Solow, Robert. 2013. Stray Thoughts on How It Might Go. In *In 100 Years: Leading Economists Predict the Future,* edited by Ignacio Palacios-Huerta, 137–44. Cambridge, Mass.: MIT Press.

Summers, Lawrence H. 2014. U.S. Economic Prospects: Secular Stagnation, Hysteresis, and the Zero Lower Bound. *Business Economics* 49, no. 2: 65–73.

Sun Tzu. 1910. *The Art of War.* Translated by Lionel Giles. At http://chinapage.com/sunzi-e.html.

Tacitus. n.d. Wikiquote. At https://en.wikiquote.org/wiki/Tacitus. Accessed July 30, 2015.

Taleb, Nassim. 2013. I Am Nassim Taleb, Author of Antifragile, AMA. *Reddit,* March 20. At https://www.reddit.com/r/IAmA/comments/1aoios/iam_nassim_taleb_author_of_ antifragile_ama.

Tetlock, Philip E. 2006. *Expert Political Judgment: How Good Is It? How Can We Know?* Princeton, N.J.: Princeton University Press.

Thierer, Adam. 2014. *Permissionless Innovation: The Continuing Case for Comprehensive Technological Freedom.* Arlington, Va.: Mercatus Center.

Tocqueville, Alexis de. [1840] 2010. *Democracy in America.* Vol. 4. Indianapolis, Ind.: Liberty Fund.

Twight, Charlotte. 2002. *Dependent on D.C.: The Rise of Federal Control over the Lives of Ordinary Americans.* New York: Palgrave and St. Martin's Press.

U.S. Bureau of Economic Analysis. 2015. *National Data: Government Reciepts.* Washington, D.C.: U.S. Bureau of Economic Analysis, June 24. At http://bea.gov/iTable/iTable.cfm? reqid=16#reqid=16&step=1&isuri=1.

———. 2015. National Income and Product Accounts, Table 7.1: Selected Per Capita Product and Income Series in Current and Chained Dollars. Revised on April 29. At http://www.bea.gov/iTable/iTable.cfm?ReqID=9&step=1#reqid=9&step=3&isuri=1&903=264.

U.S. Bureau of Labor Statistics. 2014. *American Time Use Survey—2013 Results.* Washington, D.C.: U.S. Bureau of Labor Statistics, June 18.

———. 2015. *Labor Force Statistics from the Current Population Survey.* Washington, D.C.: U.S. Bureau of Labor Statistics, February 12. At http://www.bls.gov/cps/cpsaat01.htm.

U.S. Congressional Budget Office. 2011. *Estimated Impact of Automatic Budget Enforcement Procedures Specified in the Budget Control Act.* Washington, D.C.: U.S. Congressional Budget Office.

———. 2013. *The Budget and Economic Outlook: Fiscal Years 2013 to 2023.* Washington, D.C.: U.S. Congressional Budget Office.

———. 2014. *The 2014 Long-Term Budget Outlook.* Washington, D.C.: U.S. CBO, July. At https://www.cbo.gov/sites/default/files/45471- Long-TermBudgetOutlook_7-29.pdf.

U.S. Federal Reserve System. 2015. *Strategies for Improving the U.S. Payment System.* Washington, D.C.: U.S. Federal Reserve System.

Verne, Jules. 1865. *From the Earth to the Moon.* Paris: Hetzel.

———. 1870. *Around the Moon.* Paris: Hetzel.

Wells, H. G. 1895. *The Time Machine.* London: Heinemann.

———. 1923. *Men Like Gods.* London: Cassell.

———. 1933. *The Shape of Things to Come.* London: Hutchinson.

Whaples, Robert. 2006a. Collapse? The "Dismal" Science Doesn't Think So. *The Independent Review* 11, no. 2 (Fall): 275–81.

———. 2006b. Do Economists Agree on Anything? *Economists' Voice* 3, no. 9: 1–6.

White, Lawrence H. 2015. The Market for Cryptocurrencies. *Cato Journal* 35, no. 2: 383–402.

White, Mark. 2014. *The Illusion of Well-Being: Economic Policymaking Based on Respect and Responsiveness.* New York: Palgrave Macmillan.

Whitehead, Alfred North. 1911. *An Introduction to Mathematics.* London: Williams & Norgate.

Wilcox, W. Bradford, and Robert I. Lerman. 2014. *For Richer, for Poorer: How Family Structures Economic Success in America.* Washington, D.C.: American Enterprise Institute.

Williamson, Samuel H. n.d. What Was the U.K. GDP Then? MeasuringWorth. At http:// www.measuringworth.com/ukgdp/. Accessed July 30, 2015.

World Bank. 2015a. Poverty Overview. April 6. At http://www.worldbank.org/en/topic/ poverty/overview.

_____. 2015b. World Development Indicators database. July 1. At http://databank .worldbank.org/data/download/GDP_PPP.pdf.

Yandle, Bruce. 2016. Reflections: Stagnation by Regulation in America's Kudzu Economy. *The Independent Review* 20, no. 4 (Spring).

Yankovic, "Weird Al." 2014. First World Problems (song lyrics). At http://www.azlyrics .com/lyrics/weirdalyankovic/firstworldproblems.html.

Index

About the Editors and Contributors

About the Editors

Robert M. Whaples is Co-Editor and Managing Editor of *The Independent Review* and Professor of Economics at Wake Forest University.

Christopher J. Coyne is Co-Editor of *The Independent Review* and F.A. Harper Professor of Economics at George Mason University.

Michael C. Munger is Co-Editor of *The Independent Review* and Director of the Philosophy, Politics, and Economics Program and Professor in the Departments of Political Science and Economics at Duke University.

About the Contributors

Dan Ariely is James B. Duke Professor of Psychology and Behavioral Economics at Duke University and the Founder of the Center for Advanced Hindsight.

Peter J. Boettke is University Professor of Economics and Philosophy at George Mason University.

Art Carden is Associate Professor of Economics at Samford University.

Brian F. Domitrovic is Visiting Scholar in Conservative Thought and Policy at the University of Colorado Boulder.

David R. Henderson is a Professor of Economics at the Naval Postgraduate School and a Research Fellow at the Hoover Institution.

L. Lynne Kiesling is an Associate Professor of Instruction in the Department of Economics at Northwestern University.

Pierre Lemieux is an Economist in the Department of Management Sciences of the Université du Québec in Outaouais.

Brink Lindsey is Vice President for Research at the Cato Institute.

William J. Luther is Assistant Professor of Economics at Kenyon College.

Deirdre N. McCloskey is Distinguished Professor of Economics, History, English, and Communication at the University of Illinois, Chicago.

P. J. O'Rourke is an American political satirist, journalist, author, Member of the Board of Advisers at the Independent Institute, and H. L. Mencken Research Fellow at the Cato Institute.

Benjamin Powell is Senior Fellow at the Independent Institute and Professor of Economics at Rawls College of Business and Director of the Free Market Institute at Texas Tech University.

Russell D. Roberts is John and Jean De Nault Research Fellow at the Hoover Institution.

Janet A. Schwartz is Assistant Professor of Marketing at Tulane University.

J. Walker Smith is Executive Chairman of The Futures Company.

Taylor Leland Smith is a Ph.D. student in the Department of Agricultural and Applied Economics and a Ph.D. fellow in the Free Market Institute at Texas Tech University.

Charlotte A. Twight, Ph.D., J.D., is Professor of Economics and Brandt Professor of Free Enterprise Capitalism at Boise State University.

Independent Institute Studies in Political Economy

For further information:

510-632-1366 • orders@independent.org • http://www.independent.org/publications/books/